Dear Mother,

Your first gift for you in your new home.

Enjoy both!

HOPE
≡LIVES≡
HERE

Love, Patty and Chris

xo

HOPE LIVES HERE

A History of Vancouver's First United Church

Bob Burrows

HARBOUR PUBLISHING

Harbour Publishing Co. Ltd.
P.O. Box 219, Madeira Park, BC, V0N 2H0
www.harbourpublishing.com

Photographs from the collection of First United Church and the BC Conference Archives of the United Church at 6000 Iona Drive, Vancouver, BC, except where noted. Front cover credits, clockwise from upper left: First Presbyterian Church at 152 Cordova Street, 1907 (photo courtesy Vancouver Public Library, Philip Timms, VPL 7986); Roy Stobie, Andrew Roddan and food program volunteers c.1930; homeless in the First United Church sanctuary, 2009 (Jay Black); musician and shelter volunteer "Jimmy" Kinistino (Robert Forbes); volunteers raise The People's Totem Pole, 2010 (Noel Macdonald). Back cover: First United Church at Hastings and Gore (Jay Black).
Edited by Betty Keller
Printed and bound in Canada

Paperback ISBN: 978-1-55017-520-2 / Hardcover ISBN: 978-1-55017-536-3

Harbour Publishing acknowledges financial support from the Government of Canada through the Canada Book Fund and the Canada Council for the Arts, and from the Province of British Columbia through the BC Arts Council and the Book Publishing Tax Credit.

Library and Archives Canada Cataloguing in Publication
(for paperback edition)
Burrows, Bob, 1934–
   Hope lives here : a history of Vancouver's First United Church / Robert Burrows.

Includes index.
ISBN 978-1-55017-520-2

   1. First United Church (Vancouver, B.C.)—History. 2. Church work with the poor—British Columbia—Vancouver—History. 3. Church work with the homeless—British Columbia—Vancouver—History. I. Title.

BX9882.8.V34B87 2010   287.9'20971133   C2010-904451-7

In appreciation of the life and work of
Robert Gordon Stewart
1939–2005

CONTENTS

$\equiv$ FOREWORD $\equiv$

The story of First United Church and the people who have made it a bastion of hope in Vancouver's gritty Downtown Eastside is one that has long needed to be told. There are a thousand reasons why I am glad to be able to introduce it, but to save paper I will cite only three.

When doughty Scots pioneers founded a Presbyterian church in the seaside hamlet of Granville 125 years ago, they longed for a sanctuary, a place of order, familiarity and dignity in the midst of the brawling, virtually lawless, boom-or-bust society around them. Over the years those members and their families prospered and as the settlement grew they moved to the suburbs and started new congregations. Their places were taken by immigrants from other nations whose needs were very different and, by the time of the First World War, social ministry was the primary focus of the church, which would soon become First United Church.

Rabbi Abraham Joshua Heschel used to tell his students that "when God, the Holy One, gets up in the morning, God gathers the angels of heaven around him and asks this simple question:

'Where does my creation need mending today?'" Then Heschel would continue, "Theology consists of worrying about what God worries about when God gets up in the morning."[1]

The first reason I am glad to introduce Bob Burrows' book is because of Rabbi Heschel's question. I believe that it ought to be at the forefront of the minds of all thoughtful people, whether they be persons of faith or not. Like the people whose stories are told here, our answers will be partial, imperfect and—at times—dead wrong, but in a world where money rules, where things are more important than people and where the planet itself is being poisoned, this is the central question for our time.

The second reason is that someone other than Bob needs to tell the story of his own nearly forty-five-year-long love affair with First United. Bob is at heart an entrepreneur—someone once said that if he had chosen to make money, he would be a billionaire like Jimmy Pattison. Instead, he has chosen to make money for others and give money away. He honed his entrepreneurial skills during his years as superintendent, and as a result, from the mission spun a half-dozen new organizations serving the mentally ill, the addicted, immigrants, the homeless and the poor. Now independent, those organizations continue to serve the community. In retirement he continues to offer his passion and his skills as a fundraiser *par excellence.* He has a prodigious memory. He can still tell me the date, time and place of our first meeting forty-one years ago—and the colour of tie I was wearing! In this book, as in his previous study of the United Church's mission hospitals, *Healing in the Wilderness,* he has proven to be a meticulous researcher and an accomplished raconteur. He is the right person to tell the church's story.

The third reason I am happy to write this foreword is because of my own love affair with First United. After thirty-five years of ministry in typical congregations, old, tired and—frankly—bored, I was called to be minister there. That's when I learned that the question "Where does [God's] creation need mending today?" was indeed the imperative for me, the imperative for our time.

—THE VERY REVEREND ROBERT SMITH

⇛ PREFACE ⇚

In the early 1980s the archivist for the United Church in British Columbia, Bob Stewart, set himself the task of writing the history of First United in time for the church's centennial celebrations in 1985. Bob lived in the church's apartment at that time, hosted the Saturday Night Men's Fellowship program and was the weekend custodian of this unique church in Vancouver's Downtown Eastside. He was also a member of the congregation and board as well as the founding editor of the newsletter *First Things First*. He knew this history well and, wanting to share it with others, he began organizing information and writing short sections of the story. But although a brief historical booklet was prepared in 1985, Bob was not able to achieve his goal of writing a full history of First United, and he frequently mentioned to close friends that he was disappointed that he seemed unable to organize his life to complete the task he had set for himself so many years earlier. When Bob Stewart died in November 2005, the history project seemed to pass with him.

In December 2008, First United Church initiated nightly shelter for 250 homeless people, a dramatic change in the church's life that re-kindled interest in documenting the many other re-markable changes this church has experienced. As a result, the First United Oversight Board decided that, because 2010 would mark the 125th anniversary of the church, this story should be written and, hopefully, published within that year. Since I was helping out with fund development projects on a part-time basis at that time, I was asked if I would accept the challenge of writing that amazing story—using the other parts of my time. I was honoured to be asked and pleased to accept this challenge, not least because for eight years, when I was in my thirties, I was a minister at First United, and I believe that those were the most significant years of my life in the church.

⇒ ACKNOWLEDGEMENTS ⇐

First United Church honours the Coast Salish people and acknowledges that the community of First United lies within their traditional territory.

Many men, women and children have been part of the congregation and community programs throughout this story. From the current community volunteers all the way back to the volunteers who helped build the first church on Cordova Street, countless contributions of time and talents and energy have enriched the life of the church and community. I extend a special word of appreciation to those who were members of the staff or in positions of leadership in the congregation, fine people whose faithful ministries sustained and extended the outreach to the community.

Through the past year many former members of the First United community have been generous in sharing memories and stories with me. In some cases, the children and grandchildren of former ministers have provided pictures and papers that made the story more complete. I am particularly grateful to Blair Galston, archivist for the BC Conference of the United Church, for his cheerful advice and support as I went through most of the twenty-two boxes of minutes, letters, reports and photographs stored in the Bob Stewart Archives at Vancouver School of Theology.

This project was made possible by the encouragement and support of many people. My wife, Joan, has endured once again my preoccupation with the writing of a book, and my good friend, Philip Harrison, once again made suggestions for improvements in my first draft and encouraged me to prepare a second one before submitting it to the editor. Ric Matthews and the current staff at First United Church have provided information and encouragement that have helped to shape the later parts of this story.

Finally, I express appreciation to Betty Keller, my editor. From her wide experience and gifts as a writer and editor she has helped to put clothes on the skeleton presented to her in the draft she received from me at the end of June. Bringing the story to life with her guidance has been an amazing experience for which I am deeply grateful. Betty and the staff at Harbour Publishing have improved the way the story is told. For mistakes and omissions in the story, I alone am responsible.

—BOB BURROWS

$\equiv$ CHAPTER 1 $\equiv$

1885–1916

For 125 years there has been a Protestant congregation in Vancouver's Downtown Eastside, attempting to bring hope to the people of this community. Since 1925 this church has been called First United. Before that it was called First Presbyterian Church, a pioneer congregation established in 1885, one year before the townsite of Granville became the new city of Vancouver.

During the first half of the nineteenth century, all of the Protestant churches in Canada were seriously fragmented. However, soon after Confederation, conversations began that finally resulted in the four sections of Presbyterianism uniting in 1875 to form the Presbyterian Church in Canada. Nine years later the four sections of the Methodist Church operating in Canada united to form the Methodist Church in Canada, and in 1906 the Congregational churches across Canada organized the Congregational Union of Canada. In addition, unions of local Protestant churches were established in many communities, and they formally organized as the Association of Local Union Churches.

Then in 1903 serious discussions began about uniting all of

View of Gastown from Burrard Inlet in 1884. VANCOUVER PUBLIC LIBRARY, SPECIAL COLLECTIONS, VPL 802

these denominations in Canada, but the process was slowed by opposition from a significant minority of the Presbyterians, and final decisions had to be postponed. The First World War brought the process to a complete halt, and it didn't regain momentum again until 1920–21. Then on June 10, 1925, the Methodist and Congregational churches, Association of Local Union Churches and 70 percent of the Presbyterian congregations amalgamated to form the United Church of Canada.

The early part of this story takes place, therefore, when there was already significant missionary activity in downtown Vancouver by the Presbyterian, Methodist and Congregational churches, but before there was a United Church of Canada.

The Early Years of the Presbyterian Church in Vancouver

The first Presbyterian missionary to visit Burrard Inlet was Robert Jamieson. Born in Ireland, Jamieson came to Canada in 1856 and became the first missionary sent to the Pacific Coast by the Canadian Presbyterian Church. Finding that the Reverend John Hall of the Irish Presbyterian Church was already settled in Victoria, in mid-March 1862 Jamieson moved to New Westminster. From there he made occasional visits to Moodyville and Granville, but he was primarily interested in the development of the St. Andrew's congregation in New Westminster and preaching at Langley, Maple Ridge and North Arm, near the mouth of the Fraser River. He was relieved of some of this heavy load in 1875 with the arrival of the Reverend Alexander Dunn, minister of the Church of Scotland. By 1880 Dunn was making journeys to Moodyville and Granville at irregular intervals and helping to establish a congregation at North Arm.

The Columbia Presbytery made a number of requests for more support from the national Home Mission Board of the Presbyterian Church, and that support was provided when "the Reverend Thomas Gavin Thomson, on the call of the Assembly's Home Mission Committee, was appointed to go to Burrard Inlet, British Columbia, on March 10, 1885."[2] Born in Lennoxtown, Stirlingshire, Scotland, in 1846, Thomson was a student at the University of Glasgow when his family moved to Blyth, Huron County, Ontario, in 1867. He completed his first year of theology at Knox College in Toronto in 1870–71 but returned to Glasgow to take his second year. Returning to Ontario, he served as a student missionary, but at this point he suffered from impaired health, and the Huron Presbytery asked to supervise his final year of studies. By late 1874 he had successfully completed his studies and was ordained. In 1875 or 1876 Thomson married Mary Spence, who was born in Ethel, Huron County, Ontario, in 1855. Thomson served as an effective pastoral minister

The Reverend Thomas Gavin Thomson was the first minister of First Presbyterian Church from April 1885 to November 1889. JAMES HOGG PHOTO, CITY OF VANCOUVER ARCHIVES, PORT P73

at Duff's Church, Huron Presbytery, from 1874 to 1877 and at Brucefield, also in the Huron Presbytery, from 1877 to 1885.

It is not clear why Thomson was chosen to be assigned to Burrard Inlet in 1885, as he was nearly forty years old and well established in Ontario. However, by this time the superintendent of Home Missions for Western Canada, Dr. James Robertson, who was responsible for the extension of Presbyterian missions and churches from Manitoba west, had made at least two visits to British Columbia, so there is no doubt he would have been consulted about choosing the minister to begin work there. As a student in 1867–68, Dr. Robertson had been a minister at Duff's Church and had maintained close contact with the Kerr family with whom he had lived during that year. Six years later Thomas Thomson worked closely with John Kerr, who was one of the elders in his first ordained charge, and it may have been this connection that caused Thomson's name to surface for the new missionary work on the West Coast.

Thomas and Mary Thomson began their journey to the Pacific Coast in late March 1885. Since the cross-Canada railroad had

Two unidentified men, standing near Main and Hastings in January 1886, choose the lots on which the first Presbyterian Church would be built. CITY OF VANCOUVER ARCHIVES, DIST P8.3

not yet been built, it must be assumed that they travelled across the United States to San Francisco and arrived at Burrard Inlet by ship to begin their missionary work in April. Thomson was also responsible for the young congregation at Sea Island (Richmond) and spent considerable time and energy travelling back and forth between this farming community and the village of Granville on Burrard Inlet. Beginning in May 1885, church services were held in the Hastings Mill schoolhouse and soon a congregation and a Sunday school developed.

By January 1886 the decision had been made to build a church. Three twenty-five-foot lots—40, 41 and 42, Block 9, DL 196—on Oppenheimer Street (soon to be called Cordova) were purchased from R.H. Alexander, the mill manager, for $1,000. Construction began in the spring, and by late April the *Vancouver Herald* newspaper was able to report that the "Presbyterian Church is completed, all but the internal fittings. The painters are at work on the outside and inside walls."[3] The church was opened and dedicated on Sunday, May 16, 1886. The *Herald* reported that the new Presbyterian Church "has a lofty ceiling, is well lighted, and has, on the whole, a very pleasing appearance. The first service performed in it was the singing of the 100th Psalm."[4]

Meanwhile, on April 6, 1886, the City of Vancouver had been officially created by an act of the Legislature in Victoria, and the developing city and the embryo congregation were off to a great start. Alas, just four weeks after the church opened, along with most of the new city, the church and the almost-completed manse on Alexander Street were destroyed by Vancouver's Great Fire of June 13. In 1930, seventy-two-year-old William H. Gallagher, former Vancouver alderman and a witness to events at the time of the fire, spoke at length with Major J.S. Matthews, the longtime Vancouver City archivist. One of Mr. Gallagher's clear memories conveys something of the character of the Reverend Thomas Thomson:

On Sunday afternoon—the Sunday after the fire—about 2:00 p.m., it happened on Cordova Street. Reverend Mr. Thomson, the Presbyterian clergyman, came along and suggested to the workmen who were grading Cordova Street and covering it with planks—three by twelve planks—that perhaps they ought to cease work for a moment and give thanks to the Almighty for their escape the previous Sunday. Everyone in sight laid down their tools; the teamsters left their horses standing. Then they picked up the empty spike kegs and some planks and carried them into an empty store in process of erection for Geo. L. Allen, the boot and shoe merchant, and made rows of seats out of the kegs and planks. About one hundred and fifty men went in to the service. Just at that moment His Worship, Mayor Malcolm MacLean, came along, and he joined in the simple yet deeply impressive service. The men were, of course, in their working clothes; the service was not long, and was soon over.

At its conclusion those big, rough, hardy bushmen paid as gentle a compliment as ever I have witnessed. The service over, none moved; they all stood motionless while His Worship moved down

Cordova Street, five weeks after Vancouver's great fire of June 13, 1886. CITY OF VANCOUVER ARCHIVES, STR P7.1

the rude aisle. His Worship halted at the entrance and stood to one side; Reverend Thomson on the other, and both shook hands with each member of the impromptu congregation as they slowly departed from the half-finished building. Then the men went back to work to make Cordova Street passable.[5]

Within a matter of weeks, the Presbyterian congregation, with support from some Ontario churches, had rebuilt the church on the Cordova Street site. The wood-frame church, with a capacity to seat 375 people, was dedicated, debt-free, on August 8, 1886, a mere eight weeks after the previous building was destroyed by fire.

Thomson continued to have responsibility for the work in Richmond, where a new church was also built and dedicated in July of that same year, but travelling between Richmond and Vancouver, along with the pastoral care of two growing congregations, soon proved to be more than one minister could handle. On March 2, 1887, the presbytery granted the application of First Presbyterian Church in Vancouver to become a separate pastoral charge, and the Reverend Thomson was relieved of his duties in Richmond.

The first passenger train arrived in Vancouver on May 23, 1887, inaugurating a steady flow of newcomers. In fact, in the four years between Thomson's arrival in April 1885 and his return to Ontario in late 1889, the population of Vancouver grew from 600 to more than 10,000. As a result, the congregation of First Presbyterian also grew quickly. Thomson's missionary work continued to expand and prosper until once again it became too much for one person, and in 1888 the Reverend R.Y. Thomson (no relation to Thomas G. Thomson) was appointed to assist in the work during the summer months. A survey that this young man made at that time indicated that a second Presbyterian church was required in Vancouver to provide for the population west of Carrall Street.

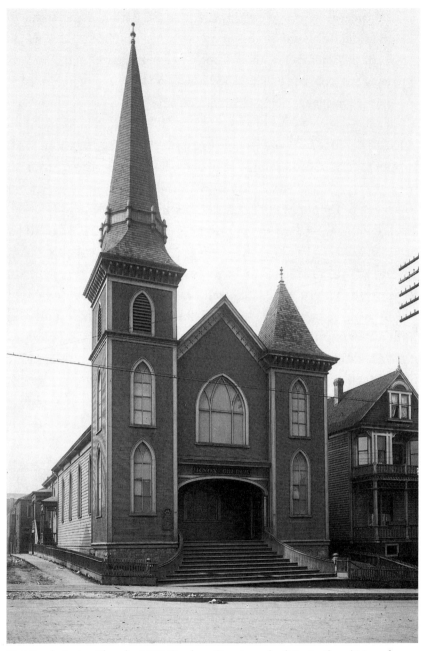

First Presbyterian Church at 152 Cordova Street was built in April and May of 1886; destroyed by fire June 13, 1886; then rebuilt and dedicated eight weeks after the fire on August 8, 1886, with a seating capacity of 375. PHILIP TIMMS PHOTO, VANCOUVER PUBLIC LIBRARY, SPECIAL COLLECTIONS, VPL 7986

The Reverend Thomas Thomson, the first Thomson, played a significant role in organizing what was to become St. Andrew's Presbyterian Church, arranging for the purchase of property on the northeast corner of Georgia and Richards streets. Then in September 1888 on behalf of the presbytery he chaired a meeting during which the new congregation was officially organized.

At this same time another Presbyterian congregation was being developed just a few blocks from First Presbyterian Church. New arrivals from Prince Edward Island wanted to have their own congregation, and the Reverend J.M. McLeod, their old friend and minister, was prepared to be their minister. When their request to be recognized as a separate congregation was turned down by the local presbytery, the determined islanders sought and received recognition from the presbytery of Puget Sound in Washington State. However, within a year it was recognized that communication and travelling challenges made this cross-border arrangement too difficult, and the congregation, now known as Zion Presbyterian Church, re-applied to the local presbytery, and this time it was granted recognition as a pastoral charge. McLeod stayed on until 1897. He was followed by the Reverend John Reid Jr., who became supply minister at Zion.

Thomas and Mary Thomson left no diaries or letters to show their perspective on their missionary adventure in Vancouver, but First Presbyterian Church developed quickly and happily during their time here. Thomson, as a good presbyter, also worked hard to establish the St. Andrew's congregation. Nonetheless, in November 1889 he accepted a call to be minister of a congregation in Waterdown, Ontario, leaving Vancouver after a ministry of less than five years. The presbytery and the congregation received this news with great regret.

In 1890 Thomas Thomson was succeeded by the Reverend George R. Maxwell, a Scottish-born and educated minister who had been serving in Three Rivers, Quebec. During the Maxwell

The building at Hastings and Gore, built in 1892, was home to First Presbyterian Church, which became First United Church in 1925.

years the congregation continued to grow, and it soon became apparent that a larger church was required. Land at the corner of Gore and Hastings was purchased early in 1892 and by late fall a new church had been built that would be used for more than seventy years. The church, with its tall steeple and a sanctuary that could accommodate almost a thousand worshippers, soon became a well-known city landmark. George Maxwell was a good preacher and pastor who inspired and encouraged his congregation as they planned and constructed the new church. These were also years of solid growth for the Sunday school and all aspects of the congregation.

There continued to be significant overall growth in the population of Vancouver during the 1890s, and the neighbourhood around First Presbyterian Church had begun to change. The Anglo-Saxon residents, who had been the city's original business and community leaders as well as the backbone of the Presbyterian congregation, were starting to migrate to the new suburbs of Mount Pleasant, Grandview and the West End. Although many continued to be members of First Presbyterian, over time they became more active in the new congregations developing in their communities. At the same time, new immigrants from around the world, and especially from Asia and eastern Europe, were arriving in large numbers, quickly occupying the houses in the First Presbyterian area that had been made available by the exodus of their first inhabitants.

Following six years as minister, Maxwell, who was not yet forty years of age, resigned and was elected as a member of Parliament for the riding of Vancouver–Burrard. As an MP, he took the initiative in getting Andrew Carnegie to fund a library at Main and Hastings, a building that continues to serve the downtown population today as the Carnegie Community Centre.

Maxwell was succeeded by the Reverend William Meikle, who came from London, Ontario. He was ordained and inducted to the ministry of First Presbyterian Church in October 1896 and appears to have endeared himself to both the congregation and the community. On the other hand, he was an outspoken critic of the larger community because of the desecration of the Sabbath, though it is not clear from the presbytery minutes whether or not his views were shared by other presbyters. Nonetheless, after only one year he submitted his resignation from the congregation; three weeks later he withdrew it. Then one year later, for reasons unknown, he did resign from First Presbyterian Church and, surprisingly, took with him glowing tributes from both the congregation and the presbytery.

At the end of 1898 the Zion congregation found itself with debts totalling more than $5,000, a situation that no doubt helped the members make the decision to merge with First Presbyterian Church. The members of both congregations were unanimous in the decision to amalgamate, and both congregations agreed to ask that the presbytery appoint Zion's minister, the Reverend John Reid Jr., as minister for one year. However, his fiery, evangelistic preaching brought controversy, and at the end of his one-year term there was a clear division among the membership whether to confirm his call. In the end the congregation voted not to confirm him, and in 1899 a splinter group of dissenters broke away from First Church. With the Reverend John Reid Jr. as minister, they used the old church on Cordova Street and became Knox Independent Presbyterian Church. Then in 1902 Knox adopted a new allegiance to become Knox Congregational Church.

Meanwhile, in 1900 First Presbyterian Church had called the Reverend R.G. MacBeth to be its minister. In his four years in Vancouver he provided steady leadership to a congregation that had been through unsettling times. However, in 1904 he moved to a church in Paris, Ontario.

The Reverend MacBeth was followed by the Reverend Dr. Hugh W. Fraser, whose preaching not only was greatly appreciated by the

The Reverend R.G. MacBeth was born in 1860 in Kildonan in the famous Lord Selkirk colony on the banks of the Red River. He did not set out to become a minister. Instead, after teaching school for one year, he attended the University of Manitoba and received his master of arts degree in 1884. He then studied law and was called to the Manitoba bar in 1888. However, after practising for just one year, he responded to a call to the Christian ministry and was ordained in 1891. He accepted the call to First Presbyterian in 1900.

congregation of First Presbyterian but also attracted many who lived in other parts of the city. One of his presbytery colleagues observed that Dr. Fraser "dominated the ecclesiastical life of the community with his rugged and frank personality, his knowledge of men and women and his direct manner of speech."[6] During his time the Sunday school flourished, and by 1905 average weekly attendance was three hundred and fifty. The congregation was generous in its support of both home and foreign missions. In fact, in 1907 First Presbyterian Church gave more than any other congregation west of Winnipeg to support mission projects, and the Westminster Presbytery recorded its appreciation.

However, despite the popularity of Dr. Fraser, the growth of the Sunday school and the congregation's reputation for generous support of missions, by the outbreak of war in 1914 First Presbyterian faced serious financial challenges. A year later, as Fraser's long ministry was coming to an end, the once-proud congregation was virtually bankrupt. On behalf of First

Hugh W. Fraser was born and raised in New Glasgow, Nova Scotia, but studied for the ministry at Manitoba College. After he was ordained in Winnipeg on March 29, 1888, he was called to be the minister at the Presbyterian Church in Fort William, Ontario, but two years later set sail for the North China Mission Field. He returned to Manitoba in 1892 to become the minister in the town of Treherne. From 1898 to 1904 he served as the minister at Brooklyn Presbyterian Church in Oakland, California; during this term he was awarded an honorary doctorate of divinity. He accepted the call to First Presbyterian in Vancouver in October 1904.

Presbyterian, the presbytery appealed for help to the national church's Board of Home Missions and Social Service, and the board agreed to assume much of the congregation's debt and guarantee the salary for the minister. This began the process by which First Presbyterian gradually became a mission-supported church, following the pattern that had developed in the heart of many of the larger cities in other parts of Canada.

Encouragement and support of many kinds were needed by the children, youth and burdened parents in the area now known as the Strathcona community. The area's low cost of housing attracted single-parent families and an ever-growing number of families newly arrived in Vancouver from all parts of the world. The church's new relationship with the Home Mission Board provided the funds to hire a social worker who could assist in the ministry to children and families. Thus, the church was well on the way to officially becoming a mission-supported institutional church.

The Early Years of the Methodist Church in Vancouver

The early history of the Methodist Church is very different from that of the Presbyterian Church. As far back as 1860, the pioneer missionary Ebenezer Robson had made occasional visits to Burrard Inlet on behalf of the Methodist Missions, but he was disappointed by the lack of interest and support from the men in the camps. The next Methodist to try to rouse the people of Granville to the church was Amos Russ, who was stationed in New Westminster from 1871 to 1875 and travelled every second week to Hastings Mill to conduct a worship service. In 1873 Russ recruited an assistant, James Turner, a young Irishman from Ontario, who assumed responsibility for the work at Burrard Inlet. In 1874 Turner built a small parsonage in Granville on the north side of Water Street, two lots west of Abbott. The front of the parsonage faced the water, and at high tide it was possible to tie canoes and boats up to the front steps and verandah. During

The Princess Street Methodist Church in 1889, built during the first year of the ministry of the Reverend John F. Betts. PHILIP TIMMS PHOTO, VANCOUVER PUBLIC LIBRARY, SPECIAL COLLECTIONS, VPL 6837

the first year, the church services, which were mainly attended by Native people from the villages around the inlet, were held in the kitchen of the parsonage.

Thomas Derrick succeeded James Turner in 1875, having previously been a missionary in the Cariboo and in Nanaimo. He had considerable success in the conversion of Native people in the area, and the parsonage kitchen was soon too small for services. The Native people contributed both money and labour for the construction of a small (16-foot by 30-foot) church on the waterfront just west of the parsonage. Derrick was followed by the reverends Cornelius Bryant in 1878, C.T. Thompson in 1881 and Joseph Hall in 1884. During the pastorate of Joseph Hall, a large hall was built on Water Street and opened for services in May 1886. In the disastrous fire a few weeks later, this hall, the parsonage and stable, and the small "Indian Church" were all destroyed. The hall was quickly rebuilt after the fire to provide a temporary place for services, but by 1888 the Methodists were worshipping in the police courts of the City Hall building under the leadership of Ebenezer Robson, who had recently returned to British Columbia from eastern Canada.

The Reverend John F. Betts became the minister in 1889 and must be given credit for finally setting the Methodist work in Vancouver on a solid foundation. Born and raised in Nova Scotia, he had taught school there for several years before becoming a minister. In 1876 he married Alice Chesley, and for the next forty years they worked together in Methodist communities across Canada. When he was transferred from Manitoba to British Columbia in 1889, his destination was just "East End Vancouver," but within twelve months of his arrival he had organized the Methodist congregation to build a church on Princess Street (the section of present-day East Pender between Main and Jackson), with a parsonage nearby for himself and his family. Reverend Betts is also credited with organizing and supervising

Looking east on Water Street, June 3, 1885. On the north side of Water Street, just west of Abbott, a Methodist parsonage was erected in 1874; services were held in the kitchen. ERSKINE BEVERIDGE PHOTO, VANCOUVER PUBLIC LIBRARY, SPECIAL COLLECTIONS, VPL 13229

the building of a new church on the corner of Main and Broadway in the Mount Pleasant district. With the normal Methodist tradition of short-term pastorates, Betts was quickly followed by the reverends W.W. Baer, R. Whittingdon, John Robson, R.N. Powell and A.M. Sanford. In 1908, during Sanford's ministry, Princess Street became officially recognized as an extension of Pender Street so the name of the church was changed to Central Methodist Church. The reverends S.S. Osterhout, F.W. Langford and J.G. Brown served from 1910 to 1915.

The Reverend A.E. Roberts was an exception to the short-term pastorate rule, serving the Central Methodist mission for seven years, from 1915 to 1922. He was born in London, England, in 1866 and came to Canada in 1889. After two years as a lay minister in Saskatchewan, he became a candidate for the ministry and was ordained in 1892. Seven years later he volunteered to come to British Columbia and served first in New Denver, then in Enderby, Nanaimo, Victoria West and Chilliwack. The challenge for Roberts when he arrived at Central Methodist Church was not only to preach and give pastoral care but to coordinate the church's social outreach activities.

The changing population within the immediate community, which had led to difficulties for the Presbyterian Church, had also brought serious financial challenges to the Methodist congregation. Like First Presbyterian, they had developed a large Sunday school and many mid-week activities for children, youth and mothers. Alas, also like First Presbyterian, they had accumulated substantial debts and needed support from the larger church. Beginning in 1914, the Women's Missionary Society (WMS) of the national church provided funding for a deaconess, a Miss Whitehead, who started a kindergarten, but it grew so quickly that the following year the WMS was called on to provide a trained kindergarten teacher as well. In October 1915 the WMS also funded the appointment of a social worker, Kate

McPherson. Reviewing her work in the Church's Annual Report for 1916, Kate McPherson told of visits to troubled single mothers, to women who spoke little English and felt lost in this strange land, to anxious women whose husbands were away at war and to mothers coping on their own with handicapped children.

From this time forward it was generally accepted that this Methodist Church would only be able to continue its work if it was provided with financial support by the national church and the WMS. To reflect the church's new character, the Methodist Conference gave permission to again change its name. The Reverend James Turner had been a missionary in Granville back in 1873 and had gone on to become a much-loved pioneer missionary in the interior of British Columbia and the Yukon. In retirement he had become associated with Central Methodist Church, and following his death in August 1916, it was decided that his name should be given to the church he had loved. The new name for this downtown mission would be "The Turner Institute," and so it remained until church union in 1925.

The Early Years of the Congregational Church in Vancouver

The Congregational Church, which joined with the Presbyterian, Methodist and Association of Local Union churches to form the United Church of Canada in 1925, began services in a hall at the corner of Cordova and Abbott streets in the new city of Vancouver in 1888. The first minister was the Reverend James W. Pedley, whose older brother, the Reverend Hugh Pedley, had previously visited Vancouver and determined that a Congregational church should be established here. James Pedley had been a minister for three years in Georgetown, Ontario, before coming to Vancouver. In 1932, one year before his death, he wrote this account of his arrival:

In 1888, I, a young fellow, landed in Vancouver to start a Congregational Church. The town was small, 2,000 or 3,000. On Granville Street there was only one small house. I rented the upper story. The Vancouver Hotel was in the foundation stage. In those days we did not confine ourselves to streets but struck out across the country in any direction . . . We had great services in the old Wilson Hall above Rand Bros.' offices [at] Cordova and Abbott streets, and later in the new church, corner of Richards Street and Georgia Street, which we put up in 1889.[7]

The first worship service was held on April 29, 1888, in Wilson Hall and the congregation was officially organized on June 17, 1888, as the "First Congregational Church." As the congregation developed, plans were made to build a church on the southwest corner of Richards and Georgia, and it was completed and dedicated in December 1889. There the Reverend James Pedley continued his very positive ministry until 1895. He was followed by the reverends H.C. Mason, J.H. Bainton and John Simpson.

When the Reverend J.K. Unsworth arrived in 1910, the congregation was still carrying a modest construction debt. With his encouragement, funds were raised to pay it off, and then plans were immediately made for a new church that would be closer to the residential area of Vancouver's West End where most members of the congregation now lived. On November 13, 1910, the Reverend Unsworth preached the final sermon in the church that had served the congregation well for twenty-one years, and on the following Sunday, November 20, the first service was held in a splendid new church at Thurlow and Pendrell in the West End. During Unsworth's ministry, the congregation continued to grow, and he was personally very active in the life of the larger community.

≈ CHAPTER 2 ≈

1916–1929

Changes in Vancouver's population, which had first become noticeable during the 1890s, were even more pronounced by 1916. As new arrivals from Europe and Asia found accommodation in the less expensive housing available in Vancouver's East End, more and more of the faithful supporters of both First Presbyterian Church and the Turner Institute moved to the more fashionable parts of the growing new city. As a result of these changing demographics, both congregations had to be saved from bankruptcy by their national mission boards. Then, because there were so many new immigrants in the area, both congregations were provided with social workers and the assurance of ongoing support for their missions.

The Turner Institute

The Reverend A.E. Roberts appears to have been the right minister to help the once-proud Methodist congregation adjust to the new reality of dependence on the national Home Mission Committee and the Women's Missionary Society (WMS) for financial support. The additional staff, which now included a deaconess, kindergarten teacher and social worker, enabled a community ministry that would have been otherwise impossible. Roberts coordinated this new mission with enthusiasm and integrity, but by 1922 he was exhausted and poor health forced him to resign. He was followed briefly by the Reverend Robert John McIntyre, and during his ministry the emphasis on sports programs continued to dominate mid-week activities. From 1923 until church union the Turner Institute's minister was the Reverend L.C. Johnson.

First Congregational Church

Although First Congregational Church had relocated to the West End from the city's east-side area in 1910, one of its ministers is particularly important for this story. The Reverend A.E. Cooke was minister at the Congregational Church from 1915 to 1924. During these years, membership doubled, congregational debt was greatly reduced, and Cooke became widely known in the city for his interest in public issues. He was frequently asked to participate in debates or public meetings to consider such topics as the merits of socialism or the moral collapse of society. In 1918, in the belief "that the press, due to commercial interests, often suppressed important news items," Cooke partnered with the Reverend J. Richmond Craig—at that time the minister at Westminster Presbyterian Church—to establish an independent newspaper called the *Western Witness,* which was to carry the news that was censored from the regular newspapers. "So hot became the *Witness*'s criticism and attacks on certain organizations that printer after printer refused to publish it, and the *Witness* ceased its existence."[8]

The new media form developing at this time—radio—showed promise in providing a fresh forum for public education. With his newspaper gone but his passion for new experiences and uncensored information undampened, in 1923 Cooke secured a radio licence for his congregation. This enabled him to broadcast church services and programs of interest to the whole community—or at least to those who had radios. The full cost of the radio ministry was paid by supporters from his congregation as well as

In 1922 Vancouver's three daily newspapers—the *Sun*, the *Province* and the *World*—all launched radio stations, although at this time not many families in Vancouver owned radio receiving sets. To spur more interest, on March 29 the *World* ran the headline "First Public Radio Concert Arranged for Friday Night" and this announcement:

> And now comes the first public radio concert in Vancouver. On Friday, March 31, pupils of the Strathcona School will give a concert in the First Presbyterian Church, starting at 8 p.m. and continuing until 10 p.m. The various numbers, including speeches by members of the teaching staff and other prominent educationalists, will be sent out over the World radio broadcasting station from the roof of the David Spencer building. It will be the first real opportunity for many residents of the city to see the possibilities of radio, for under the supervision of the Transcanada Radiovox Company a three-step amplifier receiving set, with booster magnivox especially constructed for concert work, will be installed in the church and, according to those who have charge of the work, it will be possible for those in the rear of the big edifice to hear just as well as those who are close up to the receiving set.
>
> It is to be the first real test of public radio in Vancouver, and in addition to the various numbers of the programme, those in attendance will receive a practical talk on radio by Operator Jack Wilson, the expert in charge of the World's broadcasting station. The talk will be given over the machine itself and will deal fully with radio-telephony.[9]

Unfortunately, the technology at that time was not quite up to the task at hand, and on April 1, under the headline "Radioitis Is Now Quite Epidemic in the City," the *World* announced,

> Although a mishap in the receiving apparatus made necessary the cancellation of the radio concert in the First Presbyterian Church, radio fans who were "listening in" from other stations received the full programme prepared for the concert. Mayor Tisdall, whose voice was received very clearly at New Westminster, Victoria and other points, spoke of the great advantages the radio would be to outlying districts in the dissemination of news.

The radio concert from First Presbyterian was finally broadcast two weeks later.

from the larger community. However, Cooke left Vancouver in 1924 to become pastor of a congregation in Casper, Wyoming, and within a year his radio station had been removed from the Congregational Church.

First Presbyterian Church

In 1917 Dr. Hugh Fraser accepted a call to Knox Church in Calgary, and his long ministry at First Presbyterian came to an end. (He died in Calgary three years later.) The Reverend J.S. Henderson was appointed minister for one year, with a salary guaranteed by the Board of Home Missions. He was followed in 1918 by the Reverend A.D. Archibald for a three-year appointment. The same year that Archibald arrived, First Presbyterian opened its Community House at Campbell Avenue and Georgia Street, which became the centre of a wide range of mid-week programs that drew an average of 134 participants each day. As a result, First Presbyterian began to be known as the "church of the open door," a name that aptly described how the congregation wanted to be seen by the community.

However, First Presbyterian's financial problems continued. Negotiations were

---

COMMUNITY HOUSE ACTIVITIES FOR 1924

2 White Shield Clubs (women's groups)
Kindergarten
Welfare Baby Clinic
6 service clubs for girls (6-8 years, 8-10 years, 10-12 years, 12-14 years, 14-16 years, 16 +)
Clubs for boys and gymnasium classes (Ages 8-11, 11 and over)
Sewing and dressmaking classes for girls (Ages 8-11, 11-14)
Gymnasium classes for girls and ladies (8-12, 12-17, Adults)
Concerts and moving pictures
Sports (baseball, etc.)
Hikes and picnics
Reading Room
Lending Library
Playground activities
Rummage sales
Story Hour
Dramatic classes
Planning committees for summer camps at Fircom Point, Gambier Island [10]

---

initiated at this time with the Board of Home Missions and Social Service to transfer the two church-owned properties—the Community House at Campbell and Georgia and the church at Gore and Hastings—to the Board. But the national church was only prepared to assume ownership of these properties if the congregation paid off a reasonable portion of its continuing debt. Unfortunately, raising funds proved difficult, and it was not until 1921 that the congregation finally agreed to raise $15,000 over a two-year period as its contribution to paying off the debt. They fulfilled the agreement late in 1923, and in October 1924 the properties were finally transferred to the Board.

First Presbyterian Church's transition into a radically new era began in 1921 when the Board of Home Missions appointed a new minister and added the title of "superintendent" to the position.

Richmond Craig, First Superintendent, 1921–1929

Establishing this new role was the board's acknowledgement of the First Presbyterian minister's dual responsibilities—preaching and pastoral duties on the one hand and the administration of social services and an institution on the other. The first minister/superintendent appointed to First Presbyterian was the Reverend John Richmond Craig, a man of vision, ability and remarkable energy. He possessed great gifts as a speaker, and within a few months of his arrival, the attendance at morning worship services had grown to three hundred or more. In addition, there were often a thousand people in attendance at the evening services, many of those people worshipping in their own communities on Sunday mornings. In 1923, as well as preaching twice each Sunday, Craig conducted nearly one hundred funerals and two hundred weddings.

But Craig was also a great organizer. Shocked by the crowded and unhealthy living conditions in the community, he set out to

John Richmond Craig was born in 1880 in the tiny village of Greengairs, twelve miles northeast of Glasgow, Scotland, the third of twelve children. While attending the University of Glasgow, Craig was attracted to journalism and wrote for the Scottish representative of the *London Times*, Oliphant Smeaton. When the Missionary Union of the Scottish churches decided to send an expedition to inland South America, Smeaton suggested his young friend Craig as the leader of the party. The expedition's orders were to gather all available material on the geography of the country, the natives and their languages and culture and then, if possible, Christianize them.

If Craig had any illusions concerning the ease of the task before him, they were dispelled as he was leaving the ship in Buenos Aires. The captain cheered him on his way with the advice that "the Gospel may be all right in its place, but in this country, if you get into a tight corner, use this," and then handed him a Smith & Wesson revolver.[11] Craig travelled up and down the Rio de la Plata and far into the jungle of the vast country lying between Paraguay and Bolivia. Within a year he was fluent in Spanish, and after two more years he was able to translate portions of the Bible into the Guarani language of the native people. He spent almost five years in Paraguay and Bolivia, "surviving jungle fever, malaria, native wars and several Paraguayan elections where they would shoot a few political leaders and call it a change in government."[12]

Craig returned to Glasgow in 1909 and later that year sailed to Canada aboard the SS *Grampian* with a group of thirty young Scotsmen. Following a year as a Presbyterian lay minister in Trochu, Alberta, he came to British Columbia to attend Westminster Hall for theological studies. As part of his training for the ministry, he preached on weekends at construction camps at Stave Falls and Coquitlam Lake, where several hundred men were employed constructing dams to supply water for the City of Vancouver. He also served as a student minister in the northern mining community of Stewart and then in Princeton. During the winter of 1911–12 in Princeton, frustrated with the poor attendance at church services, he wrote a brief article for the local paper indicating that the following Sunday his topic would be "Princeton's Peculiar People." The hall was almost filled that Sunday, and from that point on there was a good attendance at his services.

In 1912 Margaret Brown, the lass John Richmond Craig had left behind in Scotland, courageously travelled alone to the Canadian west, and they were married in October 1912 in Vancouver. Two years later Craig was ordained as a minister in the Presbyterian Church and from 1915 to 1921 was minister of Westminster Church, located at the corner of Sophia and East 26th Avenue in Vancouver. In this congregation his gift for preaching, his capacity for friendships and his organizing and administrative skills all blossomed. When he took on the new role of superintendent at First Presbyterian Church in 1921, he left behind a solid, self-supporting congregation.

The Reverend J. Richmond Craig, superintendent from 1921 to 1929.

give the church's social service work clear direction. He also began holding a "minister's clinic" each weekday morning from nine until noon, meeting one-on-one with dozens of people to give them advice, counselling and support. Sometimes the person might simply need a meal ticket or a bed at Central City Mission or possibly a bus ticket to return home to family in Kamloops or Victoria, while at other times there would be grave family problems to be sorted out.

He was also troubled by the large number of people whose lives were in disarray because of alcohol abuse or drug addiction. Just a year into his ministry, he organized preaching visits to the penitentiary and Oakalla Prison in Burnaby, and over the next two years he worked with a group of twenty drug-addicted prisoners. A story in the *Vancouver Province* in 1954 outlined the program:

> The men were first taken to the hospital and given treatment by Dr. A.P. Proctor. Then they were taken to a house in the West End where they lived with Dr. Craig and his wife. They were given work to do and of the 20, 12 never returned to prison. In Dr. Craig's judgment: "It's no use pampering drug addicts. You've got to cut them off completely and then fortify their willpower. My wife and I took drug addicts into our home for two years, shared their disappointments, were disappointed in them and also happy with them."[13]

Craig wanted to do something about the community's immediate needs for food, clothing and housing, but at the same time he wanted to encourage people to take more control of their own situation. His solution was the establishment of Goodwill Industries, as it was initially called, in 1923. Salvage was collected, sorted in the church gymnasium, cleaned, repaired if necessary and made available for sale. In this way, not only were many of the unemployed given work as sorters and repairers , but goods were also made available at very low cost for all who required them, although often they were given free to individuals and families who could not afford even the smallest payment. Before long, trucks were making regular calls throughout Vancouver and neighbouring communities to pick up donated furniture, appliances, household items and clothing. People came to refer to this program as First United's "welfare," distinct from its social

Volunteers and staff sort clothes in the church gymnasium in what was the beginning of Goodwill Industries, later called Welfare Industries of First United Church.

At Craig's funeral in January 1968, his lifelong friend, the Reverend Dr. Hugh Rae, told how Craig had received a phone call a few days before his death.

The caller asked if he was the preacher at the penitentiary years earlier who preached on a certain text. His answer was "Yes."

"Then," said his questioner, "I came to see you when I got out as you invited us to do. We went to consult the magistrate who did not ask for my name but suggested that I go East and start clean and new. I went, took a new name, studied for employment, started at the bottom rung, got a promotion, became manager, then superintendent of a considerable business, and now I am retired and off to California on holiday in retirement. I owe it all to you and your sermon. Thanks for everything."[14]

work or spiritual ministry, and it soon became known officially as Welfare Industries. Each year the church proudly announced how many dollars had been paid out in wages and how many people had been helped by the availability of needed goods. Annual reports indicate that 25,000 or more people benefited each year from the stores' goods.

Another product of Craig's vision and energy was Camp Fircom. He believed that many children and families in the community would benefit from a holiday away from the inner city, so he began looking for property on which to establish a summer camp. In 1923 he learned that a 50-acre site on Gambier Island was for sale. He organized a boat trip that involved a group from the congregation rowing eighteen miles from downtown Vancouver to Fircom Point near Halkett Bay. They discovered a rather rundown farmhouse on property with a small apple orchard and two beaches, an ideal location for a camping program. The program was soon under way, although the final installment of the $6,000 purchase price was not paid until 1940.

From the first year of operation, between three hundred and five hundred mothers and children enjoyed ten-day camping experiences, using tents for the first few years until cabins could be

Camp Fircom on Gambier Island, just north of Bowen Island, in the late 1920s.

The earliest cabins at Camp Fircom on Gambier Island, eighteen miles of rowing from downtown Vancouver, were built in 1928 and 1929.

The *Harbour Princess* transported campers, leaders and visitors to and from downtown Vancouver eighteen miles north to Gambier Island's Camp Fircom in the late 1920s.

built. Volunteers from First United Church and other supportive congregations helped with the construction projects. Jeannie
McDuff, a young widow who had recently arrived at First United
Church with her young son, became the camp cook, and she
continued in this role for more than thirty years.

After the end of World War I, the movement towards church
union again occupied centre stage for members of the participating churches across Canada. By 1925 it had been decided that
each congregation would vote separately on whether to unite as
one church. Craig was in favour of church union and hoped that,
because First Presbyterian's property had been turned over to
the national church, his congregation would not have to waste
time and energy debating the merits of union. However, some
members of the congregation insisted that a vote was necessary,
and after lengthy discussion, Craig agreed. The outcome of the
vote was 143 to 64 in favour of union. In late April a joint meeting with the Turner Institute, whose members had also voted in
favour of union, determined that the name of their amalgamated congregation would be First United Church and its minister
would be the Reverend J. Richmond Craig. Church union took
place on June 10, 1925, and the vast majority of the members of
the two uniting congregations became members of First United
Church.

The Sunday school enrollment was now so large that the
sanctuary and all available rooms in the church were in use.
Scores of men and women shared the Sunday afternoon teaching duties and hundreds of children participated regularly. The
annual Sunday school picnic moved to different locations each
year—Bowen Island or Stanley Park or Mahon Park in North
Vancouver—but always attracted large crowds.

In the 1920s the organization of youth sports activities was
largely carried out by the churches in British Columbia. With

A First United Church Sunday school picnic in the mid-1920s.

the leadership of a host of volunteers, First United Church developed a strong sports program that included basketball, volleyball, track and field, baseball and soccer teams that won city-wide and even province-wide trophies. In 1925 the boys' track and field team achieved seven records.

Another of Craig's interests was the radio broadcasts from

The First United Church Boys Track Team in 1925, when they won seven trophies.

47

the Congregational Church, in which he had participated with the Reverend A.E. Cooke of that church the previous year. The Congregational Church had just joined the United Church, raising the possibility that the radio licence might be withdrawn. Therefore, as soon as union became official, Richmond Craig arranged for the radio station to become part of the new First United Church. From that point on, the morning and evening services at First United were broadcast, greatly expanding the influence of the church and the many projects associated with it. The broadcasts allowed the promotion of Goodwill (Welfare) Industries, for example, and it became widely known that the organization welcomed used articles and clothing and provided jobs for unemployed people. Similarly, the broadcasts publicized the needs of Camp Fircom, with the result that more campers, camp leaders and financial donors emerged to expand the camping program.

The Reverend Richmond Craig frequently addressed controversial topics in his sermons. In December 1925, one of his sermons was a critical analysis of the Ku Klux Klan. He had been invited by the Klan to visit their "Imperial Palace" on Matthews Avenue, in Vancouver's Shaughnessy district, to discuss how the Klan could help the church deal with the drug problem. However, the day after Craig delivered his sermon, the *Vancouver Sun* reported that Craig did not want to associate in any way with a group known for its religious and racial intolerance.

In the immediate post-union years (1925–1929), Craig continued to apply his organizational skills to all the projects he had developed. He must have found it difficult to find time for other pastoral or administrative responsibilities amid the daily "minister's clinic" and the heavy load of weddings and funerals, but, supported by hard-working colleagues, his ministry flourished. It was a shock, therefore, when in 1929 it was announced that Craig had received a call to Grace United Church in Winnipeg.

The Session and Official Board tried to persuade him not to accept the call. They wrote to the national Board of Home Missions urging them to provide a manse for their minister or an increase in salary that might persuade him to remain longer at First United. In the end, Craig did accept the call.

$\equiv$ CHAPTER 3 $\equiv$

1929–1948

Andrew Roddan, Superintendent, 1929–1948

In September 1929 the Reverend Andrew Roddan was chosen to assume the position of superintendent of First United Church.

Andrew Roddan, superintendent of First United Church 1929–1948.

At the end of October, just a month before he arrived in Vancouver from Port Arthur, Ontario, the stock market crashed, unleashing events that had a profound impact on the work he had come to do. However, Roddan faced the unprecedented challenges with a confidence and determination that would define the mission of First United Church for the next two decades.

When Andrew Roddan began his ministry at First United,

MEMBERS OF THE STAFF.

MISS M. W. MORRIS.
KINDERGARTEN TEACHER.

MR. G. F. JOHNSTON.
SUPT., WELFARE DEPT.

MR. A. B. TURNER.
VOLUNTARY BOYS' LEADER.

MR. R. P. STOBIE.
STUDENT ASS'T.

MRS. H. MOSSOP.
ASS'T., WELFARE DEPT.

MRS. W. FORBES.
KINDERGARTEN PIANIST.

MISS H. A. JOHNSTON.
SECRETARY.

REV. ANDREW RODDAN.
SUPT.

MRS. J. C. PENTLAND.
HEAD WORKER.

MISS E. DEVONSHIRE.
PART-TIME GIRLS' LEADER

Staff of First United Church, Vancouver, in 1930.

he inherited a thriving summer camp, the Welfare Industries, the minister's clinic, radio broadcast services, and children and youth programs designed for both Sundays and weekdays. He also inherited Roy Stobie, a student assistant who had begun his apprenticeship with the Reverend J. Richmond Craig in 1927. Although still a student, Roy Stobie was an integral part of the staff, and Roddan was very quickly convinced of Stobie's value.

THE DEPRESSION YEARS

By the summer of 1930, the poor grain harvests on the prairies and lay-offs by government and private industry in the rest of Canada resulted in unprecedented numbers of unemployed, especially in the four western provinces where the economy rested entirely on resource exports. But the possibility of milder winters on the West Coast, coupled with rumours that work was available in Vancouver, spurred many unemployed people to travel west.

Like J. Richmond Craig and most of the other ministers who had preceded him at First Presbyterian and First United, Andrew Roddan was a Scot. He was born on July 6, 1882, in Hawick, Roxburghshire, the largest town in the Scottish Borders. He served as a lay minister with the Royal Navy at Gibraltar from 1904 to 1910, picking up key phrases in the Spanish language in addition to valuable experience working with military chaplains. He emigrated to Canada in 1910, going directly to Winnipeg where he studied for the ministry at the University of Manitoba and Manitoba College, augmented by assignments as a student minister in Saskatchewan and Manitoba. It was in Winnipeg that Mr. Roddan met his future wife, Jennie May Harrison, who was born in the small community of Niverville, twenty-five miles south of Winnipeg. They were married in May 1913 and started a family. By 1917 Andrew Roddan had completed his studies and field work successfully and was ordained as a Presbyterian minister. He served as assistant minister for one year at St. Paul's Presbyterian Church in Winnipeg and in 1918 was called to be the sole minister at Winnipeg's Home Street Presbyterian Church.

His first few months at Home Street coincided with the onset of the 1918 influenza pandemic, also known as the "Spanish Flu," and all of his enormous energy was required as he had the responsibility of conducting many funerals and supporting the grieving, frightened families. At the same time, because the congregation was growing steadily, he began creating and executing a plan to build a larger church, and for the next two years, while the new Home Street Church was under construction, his congregation met for worship in the nearby Arlington Theatre. Two former members both remembered that "it was necessary to get to church half an hour early to be sure you got a seat."[15] In 1926 Mr. Roddan accepted a call to St. Paul's United Church in Port Arthur. The next three years proved to be a positive time for him and his growing family, but in September 1929 when he was asked by the Board of Home Missions to accept the challenge of First United Church in Vancouver, he knew what his answer must be.

Soon thousands of jobless and homeless men were flooding into Vancouver, most of them "riding the rods"—that is, getting free transportation by jumping onto a freight train. Unfortunately, the rumoured jobs were non-existent. First United Church was one of the few places where the unemployed found help and food, much of it provided by local farmers, other churches and volunteers from throughout the Vancouver area. During the winter months of 1930–31, the church kitchen turned out an estimated

Roy Stobie (handing out a potato), Andrew Roddan and volunteers during the 1930–31 food program initiated by First United Church. W.J. MOORE PHOTO, VANCOUVER PUBLIC LIBRARY, SPECIAL COLLECTIONS, VPL 12748

50,000 meals; on one particular day in November 1930, by actual count, the church's workers served hot meals to 1,252 people. Most of these meals were cooked by or under the supervision of Jeannie McDuff, the amazing Scottish woman who had been cooking at Camp Fircom for some years. As a result, she soon became generally known as "the pin-up girl for the hungry and homeless."[16]

One day a leading member of the Ladies Aid told young Stobie that her husband, a city police detective, had discovered a number of men huddled in makeshift shelters on the old Canadian National Railway flats. That evening Stobie went over to investigate and the next morning reported what he had found to Roddan. Immediately, First Church, with Roddan and Stobie leading the way, began providing food for these homeless men in

Roy Stobie was born in Edinburgh and spent several early years in Manchuria where his father was a Church of Scotland minister and his mother a medical missionary. He then attended a boarding school in England while his parents continued their mission work overseas. After he arrived in Vancouver in 1925, he worked in a bank and became a member of the First United Church congregation. Two years later, he left his job to become a student assistant to the Reverend Craig, thus beginning his long journey to the ordained ministry. Believing that it would benefit both himself and the church if he had social work training in addition to theological studies, in 1928 he registered at the University of British Columbia (UBC) and became its first male social work graduate. He then entered Union College and graduated in 1936. That same year, he was ordained, married Alice Tullett and answered the call of the United Church in the mining town of Britannia Beach, which in those days was accessible only by boat.

their so-called "hobo jungle." The *New Outlook* described their efforts to feed the hungry in Vancouver that cold and wet winter:

> More than two hundred men sat down to a supper of adversity in one of the city's unemployed jungles on the railway flats east and south of Prior Street, Vancouver. There are bums in this jungle, yes; but

This widely publicized photograph shows the food line that extends from the back door of First United Church, down the alley to Dunlevy Avenue and around the corner. On that one day in November 1930, 1,252 people were served a meal.
CITY OF VANCOUVER ARCHIVES, RE N5.1

there are men here who are used to work and willing to work. Given the opportunity they would turn back tomorrow to their teaming, stone-cutting, carpentry and a dozen other trades. But there is no work of this moment; they have no money. They have sought the jungle. And at five o-clock each evening these men, after a day of wandering—looking for jobs, begging, rustling—come home to their sheltering willows and await the arrival of the noisy, efficient, old touring car piloted by Reverend Andrew Roddan of First United Church. In the back of his car he has piled the contributions of the day—bread, meat (perhaps), salt, tea, sugar and potatoes. Then they line up, this derelict two hundred, and they are joined by strays from other jungles scattered over the flats. And the food is doled out, to each his ration. There are good days and bad; fat rations and thin—but generally something. Scottish, Swedish, Norwegian, Chinese and Canadian, they are all in the same boat.[17]

There were actually four major jungle communities in Vancouver at this time, each with more than two hundred residents. They were located under the Georgia Viaduct, along the shore of Burrard Inlet, on the False Creek Flats and in the area near Prior Street. However, after eight months, the death of one of the homeless men from typhoid gave the government a reason to close down these temporary villages. To survive, most of the more than a thousand men accepted placement in the road construction camps that the BC government had set up in remote areas east and north of Vancouver.

Up to this point the Conservative government in Ottawa had been reluctant to become involved in the problem of employment, which it considered a provincial issue. However, in the fall of 1931 Prime Minister R.B. Bennett agreed to a federal contribution towards provincial public works projects that would put the unemployed to work. By the following year, the federal and provincial governments were jointly operating "relief camps," of which eventually there were 237 in BC, housing more than eighteen thousand men. They worked a forty-four-hour week, clearing bush, building roads, planting trees and constructing public buildings in return for work clothes, a bed, three meals a day, medical care and wages of twenty cents a day.

However, conditions in the camps were deplorable, and in February 1932, led by communist militants, many of the men in the camps set off on a protest march to Vancouver where they clashed violently with the police. In June 1933 the federal Department of National Defence took over complete responsibility for operating the camps, but conditions didn't improve. Soon more protest strikes were called as communist agitators within the camps organized the men into the Relief Camp Workers' Union. Finally, on April 4, 1935, the workers went on a general strike and headed for Vancouver, where they stayed for the next two months, marching daily to protest camp conditions. On one occasion they entered the Hudson's Bay Department Store to publicize their grievances to the shoppers, and when the police arrived to evict them, a bloody battle ensued. After this incident they congregated at Victory Square where Mayor McGeer came to read the Riot Act to them. Afterwards, the strikers left Vancouver to begin the On-to-Ottawa Trek, hoping to take their grievances to Prime Minister Bennett. However, shortly after the trekkers left, another communist-led strike broke out on the waterfront, resulting in a riot that became known as the Battle of Ballantyne Pier.

Roddan could not support the communist agitators, even though he admired the dedication they demonstrated. "I only wish the Christian Church could catch something of the missionary zeal which is burning so strong in the heart of the Communist," he wrote.[18] At the same time, he supported the homeless, jobless, transient men who surrounded the community at First United Church and appreciated their courage, an appreciation reflected in his book *God in the Jungles: The Story of a Man Without a Home* (1931), which was recently reprinted by George Fetherling as *Vancouver's Hoboes* (Subway Books, 2005).

But it wasn't only the homeless who suffered during these terrible years. Unemployment across the country had risen to thirty percent, and breadwinners who had never been out of work now saw their families desperate for food. For many of them, accepting the government's "relief" payments was humiliating, although this bit of money was often crucial for the survival of their families. Payments varied across Canada: for a

> **OTHER PUBLICATIONS BY ANDREW RODDAN**
>
> *Christ of the Wireless Way* (Clarke & Stewart, 1932) (a collection of 26 of his sermons)
> *Canada's Untouchables: Not Wanted* (First United Church, 1932)
> *The Church in Action* (1940) and *The Church in the Modern City* (1945) (booklets describing the work of First United Church)

> In late 1933 George Price, his wife and eighteen-month-old daughter, Barbara, were living in Edmonton where he operated two gas stations, but though he worked long and hard, he could barely feed his family. When he heard there was work in Vancouver, he packed his family into his old car and drove west. One day when he was out looking for work on foot, he heard about the meals being served at First United Church, and he got into the long lineup that stretched down the lane. When the minister, Andrew Roddan, came out of the church and shouted, "Is anyone here a mechanic?" George responded and was escorted to the place where the Welfare Industries truck stood.
>
> "It won't start," said the minister.
>
> After George got it started, Mr. Roddan asked, "Can you drive?"
>
> "Yes," George replied.
>
> "Do you want a job?"
>
> "Yes," George replied again.
>
> And from that day until the outbreak of war in 1939, George Price worked for Welfare Industries of First United Church. Then, after serving in the army during the war, he returned and worked another four years driving the truck for the "Welfare."[19]

family of five, the monthly relief cheque ranged from a high of $60 in Calgary to a low of $19 in Halifax. In Vancouver a five-member family received between $45 and $50, which had to cover rent, fuel, food and clothing. To supplement their relief payments, many Vancouver families who had never asked for help before turned to First United Church for support.

One day during a prolonged cold snap, Roddan was called to the hospital to see a baby who was dying of pneumonia. When the father told his story, Roddan wondered how many other families were going through a similar experience. The family was on relief, which at that time allowed just $3.75 per month for fuel. When that fuel was used up, the house became cold and the children took sick. The next Sunday evening Roddan told this story in his broadcast service, appealing for five hundred sacks of coal to help at least some of the families in desperate need. During the week that followed, volunteers kept the telephone line open every evening, and when the appeal was closed the next Sunday, First United Church had received three thousand sacks of coal.

By the fall of 1934 Roddan was in the midst of a vigorous campaign to clean up the city, and in his radio broadcasts and in the newspapers he described the gambling, vice and prostitution going on right under the noses of the police. Many citizens followed up on his exposé by sending letters to the editor demanding that the authorities do something about this situation. Then about one month after his campaign began, the newspaper reported the shocking news that not only had the city police raided a noisy "house of ill repute" on East Pender Street for the second time in three days, but when they investigated the ownership of the house, they also learned that it belonged to First United Church. It was, in fact, one of three houses, adjacent to First United on Gore Avenue, that the church intended to replace with a community centre for programs for boys and girls.

Sam Roddan, the eldest of the Reverend Andrew Roddan's seven children, described his father's response to the newspaper story:

> My father was speechless with anger and before even investigating the situation sat down and wrote a blistering attack on the police that was released in the afternoon papers. [Roddan suggested that the Magistrate, Mr. Findlay, was taking orders from the underworld and had deliberately ordered the investigation to discredit the church.] Then the awful truth gradually came to light. A month before, the premises had been sublet without my father's knowledge, and the evidence collected by the police was incontrovertible.[20]

After a week of tension around the Roddan home, Sam was relieved to hear his father whistling again. Later he took Sam for an evening drive to the church and happily showed him a pile of rubble where the three houses had been. This, he declared,

The family of the Reverend Andrew Roddan in the early 1930s.

would be the spot where a new gymnasium and swimming pool would be built for the youth of East Vancouver. Andrew Roddan had overridden his anger and embarrassment by taking the initiative once again. More than thirty years later, the *Vancouver Sun* published an article on this "house of ill repute" incident, quoting the Reverend Bob Henderson, then executive secretary of the BC Conference of the United Church:

> Roddan was one of the most colourful characters in Vancouver in the Thirties. On the one hand he was a very genial, kind-hearted man, a man with a hearty laugh. On the other, he spoke out loud and clear on every conceivable social problem, frequently accusing the citizens of Vancouver of gross indifference to the needs of the poor and homeless.[21]

Sam Roddan provided many of the insights and anecdotes that illuminate this story of his father's nineteen-year ministry at First United Church. He was the eldest of the seven Roddan children, and having been born before his father was ordained to the ministry, he was almost fifteen years old when the family moved to Vancouver from Port Arthur, Ontario. Sam became a writer, artist, soldier, teacher and master storyteller. Between 1970 and his death on June 8, 2002, he published more than two hundred articles in the *Globe and Mail* and the *Vancouver Sun*. A recent book, *The Best of Sam Roddan*, researched and edited by Walter Bruce MacDonald, was published by Invisible Hand Legacy Books Inc. in 2010. A copy of this book and Sam Roddan's unpublished memoirs are held at the BC Conference United Church Archives at 6000 Iona Drive in Vancouver.

GOLDEN JUBILEE

In 1935 First United celebrated the golden jubilee (fiftieth anniversary) of the church's founding, and as part of the year of celebration the congregation planned an ambitious building program. Although they were still in the midst of the Depression, the congregation boldly set out to raise $100,000 to cover the cost of renovations to the church that would comprise a community centre, constructing a separate building next door to accommodate Welfare Industries and erecting a new dining and community hall at Camp Fircom. The proposed community centre would "include a day shelter for homeless men, containing reading and recreation rooms, wash rooms and other facilities on the first floor. On the second floor there will be club rooms for mothers and children, boys and girls, and Sunday school accommoda-

In 1935 First United Church launched a fundraising appeal for church renovations and to build a three-storey community centre on its property and the property to the south. The appeal, coming in the church's golden jubilee year, was also in the midst of the Depression, and was not successful.

tion. A fully equipped standard-size gymnasium will be on the top floor."[22] But hope and boldness were not enough. The mid-1930s was not a good time to raise the funds required for all these developments, and only the new Jubilee Hall at Camp

Jubilee Hall under construction at Camp Fircom, Gambier Island, in 1935.

Jubilee Hall, which overlooks Howe Sound, was completed in 1935 and from then on, as the new dining hall, formed the heart and centre of Camp Fircom on Gambier Island.

Fircom resulted from the campaign, while the property next to the church was later sold and became the site of a BA gas station.

Camp Fircom's Jubilee Hall, built in 1935, still stands with its majestic view of Howe Sound. It has 2,750 square feet of space on each of its two floors; the top floor accommodates a thirty-by sixty-foot dining hall and a large kitchen, while washrooms, showers and program space occupy the ground floor. Andrew Roddan secured all the lumber for this building from Ralph Plante, a lumber broker who was, in the minister's words, "a good Christian man." David Spencer's Department Store (later Eaton's) donated all the appliances and fittings for the kitchen. A towing company donated its services to transport most of the building supplies to Fircom—but not quite all. After construction was well under way, twenty-year-old Sam Roddan, the eldest of the Roddan children, set out in the thirty-seven-foot Camp Fircom boat to tow a small barge loaded with bricks for the chimney of the new hall. But it was a windy day, and the tide rips near Point Atkinson were making for a rough trip. Water began coming in

The old farmhouse on Fircom Point on Gambier Island served as Camp Fircom's dining hall for fifteen people at a time from 1923 to 1935.

over the bow with every wave, and as the unprotected bricks absorbed the spray, they became heavier by the moment. Then the inevitable happened—the barge turned turtle and the bricks disappeared into the depths. Fortunately, replacement bricks were soon obtained, though whether from an insurance claim or from another generous donor is not recorded.

Another memorable event took place during the golden jubilee year, but with less satisfactory results. Gerry McGeer, Vancouver's mayor from 1934 to 1936, frequently proposed or supported policies that Andrew Roddan vigorously opposed. In early 1935, in an attempt to improve their relationship, he invited the mayor to speak at an evening broadcast service to help mark the jubilee year. However, between the invitation and the date of the mayor's participation in the broadcast, the city experienced the protest marches of the relief camp strikers, the bloody clash at the Hudson's Bay Store, the Victory Square gathering where the mayor read the Riot Act and the Battle of Ballantyne Pier. As a result, the mayor had become very unpopular among the unemployed and the striking longshoremen.

On the day of the mayor's visit, a large group of men and women packed First United Church long before the regular worshippers arrived, but they remained quiet until the mayor rose to speak. That was the signal for all hell to break loose. After a long period of shouting and screaming, the visitors filed out, the regular church members took their seats and the service proceeded in an orderly manner. However, after the benediction, the mayor and his escort of eleven police officers realized that the church was almost totally surrounded by the angry people who had been in the church earlier. So, leaving his empty limousine at the front door as a decoy, the mayor was safely escorted out by a side door. In writing about this memorable event later, Sam Roddan said that as far as he knew, his father and McGeer never spoke to each other again.

One day in that jubilee year of 1935, Orville Fisher, a member of First United Church, was sitting quietly in the church when an idea came to him, and he decided to make a proposal concerning the jubilee celebrations. As a recent graduate of the Vancouver School of Art, he suggested to his minister that he might organize the painting of murals on the church ceiling. He enlisted the cooperation of two other graduates, Edward Hughes and Paul Goranson, both of whom were—not surprisingly for artists in those Depression years—unemployed. For almost two years, whenever they were not busy elsewhere, they worked on these paintings. The three panels, which each measured twenty-five by eight feet, were entitled "Adoration," "Worship" and "Service." Another accomplished artist, the Reverend J. Williams Ogden, painted large landscapes for the lower walls of the church. Roddan, who was himself an accomplished artist and whose paintings of old ships were shown at the Vancouver Art Gallery in 1942, was very pleased and proud that the church had been made so attractive at a time when many visitors were attending special events there.

For thirteen years, from 1923 to 1936, Jennie C. Pentland was the mothers' worker on the staff of First United Church and became known as "the Florence Nightingale of the East End."[23] To single women and single mothers she was available to provide friendship, encouragement, hope and support either at the church or when summoned to their homes. Sam Roddan, writing a column about her in the *Vancouver Sun* in 1985, said that "Jennie Pentland was strong on prayers, Bible study and quilts. But especially quilts."[24] Most of them were created by the Mothers' Club, using old windbreakers, coats, vests, sugar and flour bags and remnants from old blankets, and they went to homes in the East End of the city where they were desperately needed. The warmth they provided reminded many of the special care Pentland gave

The First United Church Mothers' Club in the late 1920s.

to the weak and troubled, the lost and abandoned. She was frequently the only close support person for the discouraged, lonely women in the community; when one of these women died, she was often the only mourner at the services at Armstrong's Funeral Home on Dunlevy Avenue.

Although First United had failed to raise the money to build

The First United Church kindergarten in the early 1930s registered children from more than 20 nationalities.

a new centre for activities for boys and girls, Sam Roddan, along with scores of other boys and young men, attended the mid-week boys' club sessions at the church. The club emphasized physical fitness, so the highlight for many of the boys was the night they received a visit from Jimmy McLarnin, who became the welterweight boxing champion of the world in 1933. McLarnin had grown up in East Vancouver and was world famous for a few years. He wasn't a gifted public speaker, but he did tell the boys that being physically fit was really important. Then he showed them how to shadowbox, and before he left,

FIFTEEN-YEAR SUMMARY OF FIRST UNITED ASSISTANCE, 1930–1945

Type of Assistance	Number Assisted
Goods from Welfare Industries (household, clothing and furniture)	316,603
Employment with Welfare Industries	2,886
Counselling at church office (minister's clinic and counselling)	100,880
Counselling in homes/rooms (visits by staff members)	20,763
Funerals (in funeral homes and church)	1,659
Weddings (most in the minister's study)	3,250
Food hampers at Christmas (well-filled hampers)	8,000
Campers at Camp Fircom (children and mothers)	8,529
Total individuals assisted (primarily food, shelter, clothing)	165,465
Total families assisted (food, clothing, heaters, stoves)	47,051

Source: Andrew Roddan, *The Church in the Modern City: The Story of Three Score Years of Practical Christian Service, 1885–1945* (N.p., 1945), pp. 29–32.

looked each one of them right in the eye as he shook the hands of everyone there.[25]

There were many activities for girls as well during these years. In a letter to the First United Centennial Committee in 1985, Eveline Freethy (later Goodwin), who had been the girls' worker from 1936 to 1942, wrote:

> I was employed by the WMS [Women's Missionary Society] and my job at First United Church was Girl's Worker. I had Explorers, CGIT, a Service Girls Club, a badminton club and a group of young women called the Tonkawa Club. They were mostly young business women, but at that time many were unemployed. Then I also directed the girls' camps in the summer at Camp Fircom. It was a great time.[26]

In 1938 the radio licence held by the United Church was purchased by radio station CKWX, because the station's owners wanted to increase their station's range by switching to the church's frequency. The price was one dollar, but in return the

Current, former and future leaders at Camp Fircom, on Gambier Island in Howe Sound, enjoy a successful day of fishing. L to R: Rev. Richmond Craig, Margaret Stobie, Rev. James Mutchmor, Mrs. Craig, Roy Stobie, Mrs. Roddan, Rev. James Stobie, Dr. Catherine Stobie, Rev. Andrew Roddan.

United Church in British Columbia was to receive up to six hours per week of free broadcast time. This working agreement was sustained for the next forty-five years.

WORLD WAR II

As the Depression receded, the First United neighbourhood braced itself for the impact of World War II. Although many of the unemployed enlisted in the armed forces, some of them, still suffering from the years of privation, could not pass the physical exam and came back to the East End to exist in depressing conditions. As a result, although by 1940 the congregations were a bit smaller, there were still many single people and single-parent families coming to the church every day for help.

Roddan's enormous workload continued during the war years. He preached every Sunday morning and evening, and his evening radio audience was now estimated to number about 50,000. He provided leadership and oversight to Camp Fircom, Welfare Industries and the social service program at the church. He also averaged more than a hundred funerals each year, though most were not for church members but for people who listened to the broadcast services and were not attached to any congregation. Roddan also conducted an average of two hundred weddings each year, a number that rose in the war years, and most were conducted in his study rather than the church. His youngest son, David, tells of his own role in those weddings during the years that his three brothers and one of his sisters were away in the armed services:

> Every Saturday I was my dad's assistant, so I couldn't hang around with my pals, especially on Saturday evenings. Dad would have several weddings to perform, and my job was to keep the people sorted out in the church hall. When one wedding was finished, I would send in the next wedding party, making sure there were at least two

witnesses. Dad refused to conduct a wedding if the bride and groom had been drinking alcohol, so I was also responsible for keeping an eye on them while the wedding parties waited their turn.[27]

In the months following the Normandy invasion on June 6, 1944, First Church was involved in a project reflective of a more cohesive social milieu than we know today. The employees of the hardware supplier McLennan, McFeely & Prior Ltd., more generally known as Mc & Mc and located just a few blocks from First United, began organizing a victory celebration/thanksgiving service to be held in the church. Roddan was to preach, and the Mc & Mc choral group would lead the music. Soloists, hymns and readings were chosen and a program printed as early as September 30, 1944. The service was to be held two hours after the announcement of the German surrender or, if the announcement came after working hours, the service would be held the following morning. There were actually seven more months of bitter fighting ahead before victory in Europe finally came, on May 8, 1945, and the long-planned VE Day thanksgiving service could be held at last.

Plans for a victory celebration service were worked out in detail many months before the war in Europe ended.

During the years of his ministry, Roddan was a careful steward of First United Church's building as well as its congregation. In a report to the Board of Home Missions in January

1944, he explained what measures he had taken in the building's upkeep:

> It is a frame structure, one of the largest in Vancouver. The foundations were well and truly laid more than 50 years ago. Since becoming superintendent of this church I have made it my special business to crawl under the building and examine the beams and sills, to climb up to the roof and note any leaks, to watch the large rose windows and have them specially buttressed and girded. All the drains have been replaced.[28]

However, in spite of his concern for the church building, Roddan could do nothing to prepare it for an earthquake. On June 23, 1946, a 7.3 magnitude quake struck, with an epicentre in the Forbidden Plateau area northwest of Courtenay on Vancouver Island. Within the city of Vancouver, tall buildings swayed, gas lines cracked, a chunk of masonry fell from the façade of the train station, a fire broke out in the old Hotel Vancouver and the Lions Gate Bridge swung back and forth like a leaf in the wind. At First United Church, the impressive steeple, which was over one hundred feet tall, tipped off its base. In March of the following year, in the interests of safety, three steeplejacks were hired to remove it, and Vancouver lost its oldest spire, one that had been held together with handmade nails.

In April 1948, when Roddan was sixty-five, he was admitted to Vancouver General Hospital for prostate surgery, but his heart was too weak for the operation and he was sent home. Several days later he returned to hospital and this time underwent surgery, but he died a few days later, on April 25. Clearly, his passing marked the end of an era at First United Church. The significance of this remarkable man was captured in an editorial in the *Vancouver Daily Province* that was headlined, "He Never Compromised with the Devil."

Vancouver will never have another minister of the gospel quite like Andrew Roddan.

The big, bluff Scot with the booming voice and a vast love for human beings never wasted his time compromising with the devil.

Over the radio, in the pulpit, at unnumbered public meetings, he stood foursquare for practical, workable Christianity. Never did he stoop to say the "nice" thing when he had a chance to arouse us to our responsibilities by brusquely giving us the truth, however blunt and unpalatable it might be.

Andrew Roddan had the mind and muscles of a great Christian. He was not content to tell us what we should do. His strength, his shrewdness, his humanity showed us the way.

In the market place, in the slums and in the humblest cottages he wrestled with the devil, always demonstrating that Christianity is a religion of deeds, as well as thoughts and words.

He fought the good fight and he has finished his course. Those who take up his work have a great example and a great challenge before them.[29]

News clipping from the editorial page of the *Vancouver Daily Province*, April 27, 1948.

$=$ CHAPTER 4 $=$

1948–1968

Reg Redman, Superintendent, 1948–1954

In 1948 the Reverend Reg Redman left a successful eleven-year pastorate in Chilliwack to become superintendent of First United Church. In the shadow of his legendary predecessor, Andrew Roddan, he was undertaking a responsibility of great magnitude that involved providing leadership to a congregation and managing a social service program, Welfare Industries and Camp Fircom. Fortunately, several experienced staff members continued in their positions at the church to assist him. In addition to an office secretary and a janitor, there were staff and volunteer leaders for girls' and boys' and mothers' programs, teachers for the kindergarten and at least one community worker funded by the Women's Missionary Society.

As superintendent of First United Church, Reg[30] provided preaching and pastoral leadership to the congregation and, as had his predecessors Craig and Roddan, officiated at more than a hundred weddings per year, although he conducted fewer funerals, perhaps because he was not the radio personality that they

The Reverend Reg Redman, who was superintendent from 1948 to 1953.

had been. He devoted each morning to the minister's clinic begun by Richmond Craig in the mid-1920s, which continued throughout Roddan's ministry. The funds to make this clinic successful were secured by appeals to the generosity of listeners to the Sunday broadcast services, but the demands constantly outstripped the available money. Although the war was over and the worst effects of the Depression had disappeared, times were still tough for most people in the

Reg Redman was born on November 4, 1898, in Lower Clapton in London, England. When he was still a preschooler, his mother died not long after the infant death of a younger sister. His father, a photographer and a lay preacher associated with both the Salvation Army and the Methodist Church, took Reg and his brother to Liverpool where for the next eight years he raised his family with the active support of his mother. Never in robust health, he nonetheless remarried in 1907 and became the father of two more children. In 1910 the family of six set sail for Canada, where it was hoped Reg's father would experience better health. The family lived in Duncan on Vancouver Island, subsequently moving to Cloverdale and then New Westminster so his father could complete theological courses at Columbia College. He was received "in full connection" as a Methodist minister in 1914 but died just two years later.

To help support the family, Reg had to work, but in 1919 he began his own preparation for the ministry by first attending Columbia College in New Westminster and then studying at UBC. He completed his theological studies at Union College and in 1926 was a member of the first class to graduate and be ordained in the new United Church of Canada. He married Laura Rady, apparently the first non-aboriginal baby born in Salmon Arm, BC, and she became involved in a significant way in the life of the congregations wherever Reg served as minister.

community that surrounded First United. Reg, reflecting thirty years later on the financial challenges during his ministry, wrote:

> Dispensing these funds demanded the utmost wisdom. Many stories were heard. One had to decide which story was genuinely factual and realistic. Alcohol and drugs were devastating factors in absorbing meagre funds. . . . Amazing stories were created and told, some of which were no doubt true or at least partly true. Many poignant circumstances were revealed and it was truly distressing to have such limited resources in the face of such great need.[31]

One Saturday evening soon after his arrival at First United, Reg took a long walk through the district around the church and noted that the beer parlours were all brightly lit, warm and

Reg Redman and Harry Murphy with one of the Welfare Industries trucks.

Several of the community members surround Jean McDuff as they celebrate her friendship and her contributions of almost sixty years: Pearl Griffin, Dorothy Shaver, Winnie Mitchell, Margaret Tingley, Mrs. Oates, Jeannie, Jennie Jones and Betty Stobie (1980).

inviting. The doors of the church, meanwhile, were locked and the building stood dark and unheated. He decided it was hypocritical to criticize those who went to the beer parlours when the church wasn't offering any alternative, especially on wet, cold winter nights. So he began the program that became known as the Saturday Night Fellowship, filling the church hall with men from the surrounding community. The minister spent Saturday afternoons visiting the city's bakeries, begging for their unsold bread and cakes, and then the women of the church, as well as those from many other churches, prepared sandwiches under the guidance of Jeannie McDuff and Jeannie Kerr. The United Church Men's Groups or AOTS (meaning As One That Serves) took turns providing entertainment on these occasions, although Reg's son and daughter frequently filled the gap with their violin and piano offerings when the planned entertainment didn't materialize. This program continued for more than fifty years every Saturday night.

Camp Fircom was running well at this time, with the major challenge being the recruitment of leaders and the securing of donations sufficient to maintain the buildings and services on the camp property. However, the church's Welfare Industries was not running well. There were twenty-three full or part-time employees and a weekly payroll of $396, but the organization was $7,000 in debt and had just $51.75 cash on hand. Most of the problems, however, were due to a lack of strong day-to-day on-site management. Fortunately, in 1951 Harry Murphy, a retired businessman with experience in retail sales and an active member of Chalmers United Church, accepted the invitation to become manager of Welfare Industries for a very modest salary. For the next fifteen years, his was the public face of Welfare Industries.

Saturday Night Fellowship, begun by the Reverend Reg Redman in 1950, continued for more than fifty years as an alternative to the pubs.

Harry Murphy was manager of Welfare Industries of First United Church from 1951 to 1966.

Muriel Richardson had joined the staff in 1944 to take responsibility for the women's programs, and she remained through the first few years of the Reverend Reg Redman's time at First United. She was followed in 1952 by community worker Marion Rollins, a gentle, wise woman with a huge heart and an amazing ability to discern and affirm the goodness within each adult or child. Until her retirement in 1968, "Rollie" was for many people the heart and soul of the programs and activities at both First United Church and Camp Fircom.

In 1952 the Reverend Harry Morrow was asked by the presbytery and the Board of Home Missions to become the associate

B. Louise Foster, former overseas nurse and long-time First United volunteer, and Marion Rollins, community worker at First United Church from 1952 to 1968.

minister at First United Church. He was already well acquainted with First United as he had been a student assistant there in 1939. After his ordination in 1940, he became the minister at the United Church in Bralorne for a year, followed by two years at Williams Lake. He then served as a chaplain in the armed forces for almost three years before entering the school of social work at UBC, where he earned a master's degree. He was working at Alexandra Neighbourhood House in Vancouver when he received his call to First United in 1952.

While Reg Redman retained the major responsibility for the life and work of the congregation at First United, Harry Morrow took over responsibility for the social service and outreach programs. His presence proved especially valuable when Reg's health deteriorated in 1953 and during the transition year between Reg's resignation and the arrival of the new superintendent in the summer of 1954. However, a year later Harry resigned to become the executive director of the University Settlement House in Toronto.

Russell Ross, Superintendent, 1954–1968

When the Reverend H. Russell Ross became superintendent of First United in 1954, the Board of Home Missions was re-thinking its relationship with the superintendents of its institutional churches. Back in 1921, when First Presbyterian had begun its social service ministry with the financial support of the national church, the leadership had been clearly provided by the superintendent, the Reverend J. Richmond Craig. Although he had access to the advice and support of his session and board, all the evidence indicates that he was in charge. During the nineteen-year ministry of Andrew Roddan, it appears that the influence of the session and board had been gradually reduced even more. Then in February 1944, following a special meeting in Vancouver to consider the future of First United Church, the secretary of

The Reverend H. Russell Ross was born in September 1900 in Keswick Ridge, New Brunswick, but before entering school, he moved with his family to New England where his father, a Congregational minister, served in several churches. Russell attended the Mount Hermon high school that had been established by evangelist Dwight L. Moody, then graduated from the arts program at Princeton University and enrolled at McGill University, in Montreal, to study architecture. Before classes began, however, he changed his mind and registered in the master's program in sociology. This department required field work, for which Russell was assigned to St. Columba House, an institutional United Church serving a low-income population.

After graduation, he accepted a two-year position teaching mathematics and languages at the church-related Naparima College in Trinidad. While there, he was so impressed with the missionaries that he decided to study theology and become a minister. On his return, he enrolled at McGill's United Theological College, hoping to return to Trinidad, but by the time he was ordained in 1931 the church's Depression-ravaged finances could not support another Trinidad missionary. Instead, he began his career as a minister in the thoroughly un-tropical Peace River country, responsible for churches at Pouce Coupe and Dawson Creek. While there, he met a schoolteacher named Jean Crosson, whom he married on June 30, 1933.

Pastorates in Leduc and Red Deer, Alberta, followed. During the war he served as an RCAF chaplain and then in 1946 became minister of Trinity United Church in Calgary. This church, located in that city's industrial East End, had recently become an institutional church, its budget supported by substantial grants from the Board of Home Missions, and it proved to be an excellent training ground for the years ahead when Mr. Ross became superintendent of First United in Vancouver.

the Board of Home Missions, Dr. George Dorey, came to the conclusion that too much authority resided with Roddan. Dr. Dorey suggested that an advisory group be established to work with the superintendent, although he was very careful to word this as a recommendation, not a requirement. Probably as a result of his caution, his recommendation was ignored or forgotten until eleven years later, one year after the arrival of Russell Ross. At that time, the Vancouver Council for Institutional Work was created to provide oversight, advice and support for all of the ministries and projects under the supervision of the superintendent of First United. The advice that grew out of the new council's quarterly meetings was much appreciated by the new incumbent.

Superintendent Russell Ross joined the Reverend Harry Morrow, Home Mission worker Marion Rollins and several other staff members to minister to a shrinking but still substantial congregation. By that time the flood of post-war immigration that had poured tens of thousands of new Canadians into the country had become very evident in the East End

The Reverend Dr. H. Russell Ross, who was superintendent of First United Church in Vancouver from 1954 to 1968, led the rebuilding project in 1964–65.

of Vancouver. First United provided support for many of these newcomers, even creating small congregations of Dutch, Finnish, German, Japanese and Ukrainians who worshipped in their own languages. The ministers assigned to each of these congregations were all accountable to the superintendent of First United, even though their worship services and offices might be located elsewhere. The emphasis on this ethnic ministry was at its peak in the years of Russell's leadership.

Meanwhile, service to single men and low-income families was still a major part of the First United ministry. The "minister's clinic" was now replaced with counselling and support from community workers, who were available every day for single men and for women and families. Each morning lineups formed with men and women seeking advice, clothing, groceries, sandwiches and coffee. The Saturday Night Fellowship established by Reg Redman continued to be packed with more than two hundred men each week, while the mid-week Happy Hours program served seniors effectively with the many volunteers who came from other churches with food and entertainment. The Cub and Scout programs were both well organized during this period and represented the church's most effective outreach to youth in the Strathcona community.

Two volunteers with special roles during the 1950s and 1960s, Connie Stinson and B. Louise Foster, worked quietly and efficiently in the church office. For more than thirty years Connie came in every Tuesday to help with a variety of office tasks to relieve the pressure on the regular staff members, and B. Louise, a retired China missionary, personally wrote letters to all of the radio listeners who supported the church with donations. These two women were fine examples of the intense loyalty and support First United Church received from the wider church and community.

The superintendent of First United Church also acted as the president of Welfare Industries of First United Church Society. Russell Ross took this responsibility seriously and gave considerable time and moral support to Harry Murphy, the manager, as this program went through growing pains. It seemed that each year saw a few more people employed, more goods sold, another new store opened, and a new truck obtained, as more churches supported Welfare Industries by collecting suitable donations of clothing and other articles. In 1956 the warehouse was relocated to 111 Victoria Drive and ten years later it received a 17,000-square-foot addition. Harry Murphy retired a few months later; by this time there were seven retail stores in Vancouver and Burnaby, a fleet of four trucks picking up clothing and other used articles, and forty-five employees, many of whom would have had difficulty finding employment elsewhere because of handicaps or other challenges. When he started Welfare Industries in 1923, Richmond Craig had said, "You can't

Most of the Welfare Industries staff are shown here at the official opening of the new addition to the warehouse at 111 Victoria Drive, Vancouver, in 1966.

tell people to go to someone else for help. You've got to help them yourself, and to do that, you have to offer them a job where they will be paid at the end of the day." Four superintendents— Craig, Roddan, Redman and Ross—had all seen the wisdom of these words, each having his own effect on this program, and because of it, low-income people throughout the Lower Mainland were able to purchase goods at very little cost.

In 1968, the final year of Dr. Ross's tenure (he had received an honorary doctor of divinity degree in 1960), a non-profit organization called the Vancouver Training Workshop for the Handicapped made a proposal to purchase Welfare Industries of First United Church. This organization had professionally trained staff who worked with young adult handicapped men and women. They needed a workplace environment for their clients, and many of the jobs at Welfare Industries were deemed suitable for their work. The provincial government had promised to provide funding and the Vancouver Foundation had also pledged substantial financial support if they could purchase a facility that would permit the expansion of their program. In effect, their offer was to continue the work of Welfare Industries and to add a training component the church had not been able to provide. Although it was not an easy decision to make, the Welfare Industries of First United Church Society agreed to the sale in May 1968, hoping that an even greater community service would be possible in the future. To provide continuity and show the continued commitment of First United to the people and the goals of the new program, First United's superintendent served on the Board of what was now called the Opportunity Rehabilitation Workshop (ORW) from 1968 to 1972.

Another major role Russell Ross inherited was superintendent of Camp Fircom, the church's fifty-acre, fresh-air camp on Gambier Island. While the programs of the camp were operating well when he arrived in 1954, many of the buildings were in need of repair or replacement. In 1957, a decade of building activity at Fircom began, with the assistance of women's groups at First United, couples' clubs from North Shore churches, the AOTS men's groups, and the newly formed Institutional Council Auxiliary, which had been established in 1956 following the creation of the Institutional Council. Old cabins were replaced and a picnic shelter and barbeque fireplace installed. In 1967 a twelve-room dormitory (two beds per room) was constructed for summer staff, although it was also suitable for year-round camp groups. It was named "Craigcroft" in honour of the camp's founder, Dr. Craig, who was thrilled to be present for the building's dedication in September 1967.

Another action Dr. Ross took, though little known, resulted in a significant enhancement to Camp Fircom. In 1960, when the Gambier Estates development was under way adjacent to the Camp Fircom property, he learned that a twenty-two-acre parcel of land adjoining the camp was available for $15,000, and he

Junior Boys at Camp Fircom in 1967.

Summer staff at Camp Fircom on Gambier Island, northwest of Vancouver, in 1970. Top row, L to R: Greg Johnson, Chris Ferguson, Victor Cumming, Al the cook, Scotty the maintenance man and Bob Burrows.

realized that it would provide an excellent buffer between the camp and potential cottage properties. It happened that First United had just received an unrestricted bequest of $5,000, and in a matter of days Mr. Ross had secured the agreement of the Board of Home Missions to match that amount from national mission funds. Over the following six months, church and camp supporters donated enough to cover the rest of the purchase price.

In 1985, thinking back to his years at First United, Dr. Ross wrote:

> Possibly the most exciting part of my ministry was the live radio broadcast on CKWX of the Sunday evening service from our church sanctuary. It was estimated that there were 30,000 listeners spread from Oregon to the Yukon and from the Queen Charlotte Islands [now Haida Gwaii] to Saskatchewan. The live broadcast required that every minute be accounted for, with no "dead spots."[32]

In fact, not only had every minute to be fully used, there was also a one-minute warning light that frequently cut short the sermon or the final hymn. The church choir, augmented for many years by a professional quartet, was also important for the broadcast services.

Although no formal appeal for funds was made on these broadcasts, throughout the year many listeners sent donations to support Camp Fircom or the social service work of the church. However, an annual appeal letter was sent out to bring in donations from individuals and churches for the Christmas Cheer Fund, which supported First United's work at Christmas and throughout the year. These donations represented approximately 10 percent of the budget for the church's social service ministry.

Throughout this period, the church building at Gore and Hastings was in dire need of attention. It had lost its steeple after the earthquake in 1946, and when Russell Ross had first arrived as superintendent in 1954, he had noticed that bricks from the church's chimney occasionally fell onto Gore Avenue. By 1959 it seemed that the whole building was in need of drastic renovation or complete replacement. There was also an urgent need for additional space for the ever-expanding social service program, for chapels or extra worship space for some of the ethnic ministries, a modern, functional kitchen and a larger gym or hall for athletic programs. Although these needs had been expressed many times before, Russell Ross took action, explaining his concern about the inadequacy of the church building to the new Vancouver Council for Institutional Work. Fortunately, they took his concern seriously, and with their encouragement, in 1959 he presented a proposal for a new church building to the presbytery. It was not until 1962, however, that the support of

First United Church in 1958, without the steeple and with the addition of the Social Centre directly east of the church.

The First United Church Social Centre was built on the property next door to the church on Hastings Street.

the churches and the Board of Home Missions crystallized. The funding objective was $500,000, and a campaign to secure it was coordinated by John M. Buchanan, the recently retired president of BC Packers who was also a member of the University of British Columbia senate and soon to become the university's chancellor. The objective was reached with a gift of $175,000 from the P.A. Woodward Foundation, $70,000 from the property fund of the Board of Home Missions and the balance from individuals and congregations.

Margaret Fulton, who had joined the staff in 1962 as a WMS worker and was responsible for Christian education programs both Sundays and mid-week as well as counselling with women and families, later recalled the excitement of the hectic pre-construction period:

> For us on staff in the early sixties, the building of the new Church was an exciting project to be involved with. . . . There were many meetings with the architect, and staff had some opportunity to

give their ideas. Marion Rollins was adamant that the office area must have washroom facilities.

In April 1964 all of First United's programs and services were transferred to the big Ukrainian Hall at 604 East Cordova Street, a hall that Margaret Fulton would later remember as being extremely cold. The 1892 church building was then demolished. This apparently happened just in time, because, Fulton recalled, "one Sunday during the last days in the old building, the ceiling of the narthex fell down—a sure omen that a new building was needed." [33]

In just under one year, services of dedication and thanksgiving were held in the new First United Church at Gore and Hastings. The building, which was designed to meet the current and anticipated future needs of the community, was dedicated on March 5, 1965, with its "official opening" services on March 14. Two former ministers, the reverends Reg Redman and Dr. J. Richmond Craig, were the guest preachers at homecoming services on March 21, 1965.

Following the departure of the Reverend Harry Morrow in 1955, Russell Ross had been joined by several associate ministers who shared the preaching and pastoral responsibilities with him: Reg Brown, David Matheson and Bruce Cameron. I followed them as assistant superintendent/minister in 1966 and for the next two years had the privilege of working closely with Dr. Ross and the other members of his team, which included Marion Rollins, Margaret Fulton, Muriel Richardson, Gail Risdill, Ralph and Jennie Jones, Joan Birchall, Pearl Willows, Pat Clarke and Margaret Maxwell.

I arrived at First United at a time when the United Church was looking for ways to make its urban institutional mission more effective, and it just happened that I had been reading about

The Reverend Bob Burrows, who was superintendent of First United Church from 1968 to 1974.

the special outreach mission projects in Chicago and the programs of the East Harlem Protestant Parish in New York. The project in East Harlem had been initiated in 1948 in an effort to make contact with the people in that district who had no church connections because all the downtown Protestant churches had closed. Since that time, the writing and public presentations of the project's three leaders—George Webber, Archie Hargraves and Kilmer Myers—had caused a re-thinking of approaches to mission work in the heavily populated, poverty-stricken inner cities right across the continent. The Board of Home Missions, knowing of my interest in that work and knowing I planned to be on vacation in Ontario during July 1966, encouraged me to take two additional weeks and see first-hand what was happening in these missions as part of my orientation to my new job. In a sense, the church was investing in me.

Meanwhile, meetings had been taking place among clergy and other workers in Canada's Anglican, Presbyterian, United and Roman Catholic churches to consider new ways to approach ministry in inner-city communities. A decision was reached in 1965 to create a new training program for ministers working in urban situations, to be called the Canadian Urban Training Project for Christian Service (CUT). To finance it, each denomination paid a percentage of the budget plus a fee for each participant. The first six-week program was held in Toronto in the

Bob Burrows grew up in a small Scarborough village called Agincourt, twenty-four kilometres from downtown Toronto. As a young man he was seriously involved in music, sports and the church youth group. He worked as a cost accountant at IBM's head office in Toronto for two years but left in 1953 to attend the University of Toronto in preparation for the United Church ministry. Following graduation from Emmanuel College and his ordination in 1959, he married Joan Fidler, and together they went to St. Andrews, Scotland, where he studied on a post-graduate scholarship while Joan taught school.

In September 1960 Bob Burrows became the missionary/captain of the MV *Thomas Crosby IV*, based at Ocean Falls, BC. His work involved visiting fifty isolated central and north coast settlements—isolated lighthouses, Native villages and logging and fishing communities. Two years later the Board of Home Missions transferred him to Alert Bay where he learned to pilot the Cessna 170 float plane *George Pringle*, which took him and his ministry to some fifty ports of call near the north end of Vancouver Island. In both these posts he worked closely with First Nations people and in the process came to appreciate their cultures and traditions. In 1966 he was called to be the assistant superintendent/minister of First United Church in Vancouver.

fall of 1966. I was a participant in the second program, which ran from January 30 to March 12, 1967.

My CUT classmates were several other United Church and Presbyterian ministers and one Roman Catholic priest. The Reverend Dr. Edgar File was the director of the project, and he had recruited several resource leaders from the Toronto community. Week one began with orientation and preliminary lectures, and then on Thursday evening key business leaders hosted a dinner for us at the exclusive Albany Club. On Friday morning we were all sent out the door, unshaven and shabbily dressed, for a three-day "plunge" of living on the cold Toronto streets with only $5 for our expenses. It was bitterly cold, and I quickly discovered that there were few places where shabby-looking men and women were welcome. Even at bus and train stations we were urged to vacate the waiting areas, and I knew that back home in Vancouver, even though the temperatures were never quite as low, the reality was much the same. People who spend most of their time on the streets have few places to go where they are welcomed. This experience of "the plunge" had a profound impact on me and ultimately on projects associated with First United Church.

The following Monday we began our five-week field placements, which had been arranged to provide us with significant involvement in agencies such as the Social Planning Council and the headquarters of the Toronto Police Department. My placement was at Toronto's city hall in the office of the city clerk, where I was involved in the city's daily administration and learned how changes in policy were implemented.

When each of the CUT participants returned home, we were required to record our success at putting what we had learned into action. I began that process in October 1967 by sharing my plunge experiences at a regular meeting of the Downtown Eastside Clergy Association, which met monthly for both fellowship and strategic planning conversations about our shared concerns for the people in our downtown community. I made a proposal to them that we try to create a warm, safe, welcoming drop-in centre for people who live in the tiny rooms and hostels of that area and have no "living-room." The group encouraged me to move forward with this idea, assuring me of their support. Within a few days we had rented the storefront space of a four-storey Powell Street building, and when this was announced at the Saturday Night Fellowship a few days later, six men volunteered to help with the necessary renovations.

For two months these enthusiastic men worked part of each day scraping, painting, planning and building. Then one day from high up on a ladder Bruce called down to me, "Bob, who's going to run this place when we open up?"

"Volunteers," I said. "I don't know who they will be but we'll find some. Why do you ask?"

"Well, me and the boys, we've been talking. We think we'll need a doorman to keep out people who are not in good shape and would spoil it for everyone else. Larry's willing to do that. And Tom, he's pretty shy but he says he'd like to do the clean-up at night after everyone's gone. And Paddy, Bob, Ralph and I can make and serve the coffee."

After all these years I don't remember exactly what my immediate response was, though I know I was pleased. For almost forty-three years now the drop-in centre has been staffed by volunteers from the community, and the whole operating philosophy came not from the clergy but from members of the community.

We needed a name for our drop-in centre, and when I contacted my friend Art Hupy, a photographer who was experienced

Four of the six original volunteers in 1967, who worked for six weeks that year scraping and painting and building to transform a warehouse into the Dugout Drop-In Centre. They then decided that they would be the volunteers who would run the Dugout when it opened, and they did. L to R: Tom Boston, Ralph Sayer, Bruce McQuarrie and Dennis Davison. BILL CUNNINGHAM PHOTO, *VANCOUVER PROVINCE*

in the advertising industry, he suggested "The Dugout." In the two world wars the dugout had been the place where soldiers went to escape the harshness of the battle, get some nourishment and prepare to go back to the front lines. And so it was that the Dugout Drop-In Centre opened its doors on December 9, 1967; it has been open every day since. Sid Lane, a retired business-man and AA veteran, was engaged as our part-time manager, and under his initiative a daily Alcoholics Anonymous program began meeting at the Dugout in April 1968 and still continues to bring together people who work downtown as well as those who live in the area.

However, within two years of the Dugout's opening, "Gastown" was rediscovered. Old buildings were restored. Boutiques, res-taurants, and stores of all kinds sprang up, and many of the mer-chants were not happy about the Dugout because it attracted low-income visitors who were not buying in their shops. Then in the late 1970s, the Dugout's building was listed for sale, and we were advised that some merchants were pleased that they would now get a chance to buy the building and get rid of the Dugout. Fortunately, the City of Vancouver, encouraged by its Social Planning Department, purchased the building so that the Dugout wouldn't lose its space. This also gave the city the op-portunity to renovate and improve the quality of the thirty small housekeeping rooms on the three upper floors.

Although the Central City Mission, St. James Anglican Church, Holy Rosary Cathedral and First United Church were the initial financial sponsors of the Dugout, it is currently sup-ported generously by Central City Foundation, First United Church, Anglican churches, many private individuals, and espe-cially by the City of Vancouver. In fact, at every level, from the first application for a permit for the Dugout in November 1967 through June 2010, the Dugout has provided a wonderful exam-ple of civic servants using their influence to help a community cause. The City of Vancouver has been an amazingly supportive partner in this program.

The CUT training program had also encouraged consultation between churches and community agencies. "Don't do anything on your own that you can do with others," they told us, and "Don't duplicate anything that is being done well by another church or agency." This wasn't necessarily a new idea, but the CUT program reinforced it and taught us how to find the tools to implement some new strategies for our urban missions. It also showed us how to look at the power structures in our own cities so that we could better understand where to apply pressure for changes that would improve the situation for low-income people.

The Vancouver Inner-City Service Project, which was launched in 1967 with First United Church playing a significant role, was a good example of putting these strategies to work. Its genesis occurred in September 1966 when Gordon How, a theological student at Union College, came to see me just as I was adjusting to my office and work at First United Church. He had been a student minister in rural Alberta for four months and expressed the hope that the following summer he might have a student field placement in Vancouver. What did I think? From that small beginning, many others joined in the discussions. They included the Reverend Val Anderson, who was a new member of the Union College faculty; the Reverend Jack Shaver, the United Church chaplain at UBC; and the Reverend E.M. (Ted) Nichols, who was on staff at Union College but was also a former staff person for the Student Christian Movement (SCM), an organization with years of experience bringing together university students for summertime community work camps.

Over the next few weeks, many others participated in planning meetings, and by mid-November we had agreed that what we were striving for was a four-month summer project involving theological students along with students from engineering, medicine, social work, arts and law, hopefully sharing in programs that worked with children and youth in the West End, the East End of Vancouver near the Skeena Housing Project and the Downtown Eastside community surrounding First United Church.

Then in late November we received notice from Dr. J. David McGann, a professional consultant with the Vancouver Foundation, that within a few days there was to be a meeting of a charitable foundation that had funds to distribute, especially for youth-oriented projects. That Sunday afternoon ten people sat around our dining table trying to draft a grant application for the Monday morning deadline. At the conclusion of our meeting one of those people said, "My wife can type. I'll take it home and ask her." He left the typed application with me early the following morning, and with my three-year-old daughter in tow, I dropped off the proposal at a downtown office five minutes before the deadline. Four days later David McGann phoned with the amazing news that the Spencer Foundation had approved a grant of $3,750 to fund three students for our summer project, and the Vancouver Foundation had decided to match this amount. (Between the years 1966 and 1974, Dr. McGann also helped to facilitate Foundation grants to the Dugout, Camp Fircom, United Church Health Services and several other projects in which First United Church was involved.) By mid-December the national office of the United Church had approved a $10,000 grant from its new Experimental Ministries Fund, and by March we knew we had sufficient funding for twenty-two students and the commitment of the SCM to provide ten students to associate with the project and live in residence with our students.

The vacated Columbia Street United Church at Sixth and Columbia and the adjoining manse provided accommodation for the students. During the day they worked with children and youth, usually in programs operated by churches or social agencies in the West End, the Downtown Eastside and the Skeena Housing Project. Evening sessions brought evaluation and stimulating discussions, often with external resource leaders from the wider community.

The Reverend Jim Taylor was the director of the project in 1967. He had just resigned from East Burnaby United Church and was moving to Calgary in September to be a hospital chaplain. As an experienced, mature minister and trained counsellor who had always been on the cutting edge of adventurous new approaches to church and community projects, he was uniquely qualified to both direct this project and provide personal support to students as they struggled with their respective challenges. Clergy from the areas where the three teams worked became their supervisors, meeting weekly with them and encouraging them to express their concerns and their triumphs. The project's crowning achievement, of the many positive experiences emerging from it, was that many of the participating churches and agencies became convinced of the value of inter-agency cooperation.

Although the main thrust of the project occurred during the four-month university vacation period, staff energy was needed throughout the year, at least on a part-time basis. In 1968 R. Max Beck was hired as the year-round half-time director of the Inner-City Service Project. He was able to arrange another half-time contract, this one with the UBC School of Social Work, to supervise five students working with community development projects. He balanced his time by giving all of his energies to the Inner-City Service Project in summer and approximately 75 percent of his time to his social work responsibilities in winter; thus we had the services of a top-of-the-line expert for the next four years. For each of those summers from 1968 to 1972, between twenty and twenty-five students participated in the four-month project. Numerous new projects developed from their creativity and initiative. In 1969 as Inner-City Service Project activities were expanding, Michael Harcourt was hired as assistant director. Mike, a young lawyer at that time, was advocating store-front law offices, and he brought new ideas and energy to the summer program as well as special year-round leadership.

Since I was the chair of the organizing committees for both the Dugout and the Inner-City Service Project right from their beginnings, they demanded a large portion of my time. Despite the fact that much of this was Monday to Friday time, I was still able to share the preaching and pastoral work with my colleagues, become significantly involved in the work of Camp Fircom and Welfare Industries—and even managed to have supper with my family most nights. It was typical of Dr. Russell Ross that despite the amount of time I was giving to the new projects, he gave me generous encouragement and support to pursue them. The transition to the next chapter in the First United Church story was already under way.

$=$ CHAPTER 5 $=$

1968–1975

In 1968 First United Church was the largest of the urban institutional missions supported by the United Church of Canada,
with two-thirds of its budget provided by the Board of Home
Missions. This financial arrangement was not unusual; most of
the institutional churches across Canada operated in much the
same way, although each mission adapted its activities to local
needs. However, over the years the manner in which the missions spent their budgets had changed. During the Depression,
the churches had responded with charity to relieve the desperate and immediate needs of the poor and homeless. Little time
or attention had been given to the root causes of the hardships
these people were experiencing. This approach had gradually
changed during the post-war years. Since 1965, in an attempt to
increase the positive impact of the missions, the Board of Home
Missions had been supporting the Canadian Urban Training
Project (CUT) and sponsoring clergy and community workers
to participate in it in the hope that this training would bring
more positive changes on the front lines.

At First United, just as the work of the mission was beginning to evolve to reflect the changing needs in the community, half the staff was about to change, too, due to retirements and furloughs. In early February 1968, Dr. Ross submitted his resignation, to take effect June 30. Marion Rollins and Muriel Richardson announced their retirements for that same date, while Margaret Fulton, a WMS worker coming up to her furlough year, was also scheduled to leave on June 30. Then in March I received a letter from the Board of Home Missions asking if I would accept the position of superintendent. This was not a total surprise, but it was the first time a superintendent had been appointed from within the existing staff.

Bob Burrows and the Team, 1968–1974

My appointment as superintendent was confirmed in early April. The staff members who would remain after the end of June were diaconal minister Pearl Willows, men's worker Owen McPherson, and Camp Fircom manager Ralph Jones. The word "busy" is inadequate to describe the next few months, during which we prepared to acknowledge the faithful ministries of those who were leaving and recruited new staff members who would not merely be good at their jobs but would want to work in a team ministry.

The Reverend Glen Baker was called to be assistant superintendent/minister. He had served as a pastor in McBride, BC, and at South Arm in Richmond and had a special interest in pastoral counselling. In addition, the team was enhanced by the appointment of Elsie Rosenberg, a diaconal minister who had been doing community work in Vancouver's West End with the Reverend Roy Stobie; Judy Langdon, a recent graduate of the UBC School of Social Work who had a special interest in youth work and camping programs; and Linda Malila, a German language teacher with international experience.

It had been established practice in most of the United Church urban missions that a respected, mature superintendent would operate as a chief executive officer. Drs. Craig and Roddan had been cast in that mold. They were men of their time and the right men for the job—forceful and effective leaders when forceful leadership was indispensable. Neither they nor anyone around them was ever in doubt about who was boss. By the late sixties, however, both the changing and increasingly varied nature of the work at First United Church as well as the temper of the times called for a more collegial form of administration. As a result, the creation of a genuine team structure was a primary objective of our new administration from its inception. We were attempting to break the former pattern and, I believe, we were at least partially successful; although the buck still finally stopped at the superintendent's door, we were usually able to reach consensus decisions on important issues before action was taken.

Every Friday afternoon we met as a team to review what each person was doing, to give support to one another, to put our ideas and hopes on the table for consideration, to celebrate the good things that were happening and to air our frustrations and disappointments. We took turns chairing the team meetings and acting as secretary; following one month of taking minutes and one month of chairing the team meetings, each team member could look forward to several months free of these responsibilities.

From the beginning of our time together we were committed to programs and relationships that would help individuals and families stand on their own feet and make their own decisions rather than rely on the well-intentioned charity of others. We tried to encourage people with alcohol addictions to become associated with Alcoholics Anonymous and families struggling with inadequate social assistance payments to participate in community support groups where nutrition and budget planning were emphasized. What we did not believe was that we were called to duplicate the soup lines that were provided by other

The First United Church downtown ministry team looks out over their parish from the corner of Hastings and Gore, August 9, 1972. L to R: Gail Price, Rev. Bob Burrows, Ross Henry, Kathy Anderson, Peter Davies (with beard), Joe Cannon and the Rev. Glen Baker. PHOTO: TC 72-2577 VLAD KEREMIDSCHIEFF/*VANCOUVER SUN*, PNG MERLIN ARCHIVE

downtown agencies. Rather, we believed that we were called to stand with the members of our community as they went through their struggles. At the centre of our mission was the intention to provide hope for a better life.

The new team members, in addition to getting to know the City of Vancouver, First United Church, Camp Fircom and other community agencies, had to get to know one another better, so once or twice each year we arranged for a retreat led by an outside resource person. We were able to celebrate the things that had gone well, learn from a review of things that had not gone well, consider future possibilities and assign leadership roles for each area of our work. This was also an opportunity for a team member to ask to be relieved of a responsibility, and some shuffling of assignments usually resulted from this process. These sessions proved invaluable as we faced the possibility of several new projects each year.

One of our objectives as a team was to create an atmosphere where the members felt comfortable and free to raise their suggestions or concerns. In the spring of 1969 Linda Malila put forward an idea for a summer enrichment program for the children living in the Strathcona community. It had the potential to involve hundreds of children and scores of volunteer leaders, and the team was a little skeptical that it could be pulled off, but we encouraged her to run with the idea and see what happened. By collaborating with Pauline Topp of the Pender YWCA and securing the assistance of social planner Darlene Marzari, Malila developed a blueprint for six weeks of five-days-a-week activities. When the Citizenship Branch of the federal government provided a grant that helped to finance the program, the Strathcona Summer Enrichment Project became a reality. Three hundred and fifty children, many of them new Canadians, and forty-five volunteer leaders, many of them university students unable to find paying jobs, became involved that first summer. Recreation and craft programs were held in local churches or agencies, and the children were taken on field trips to parks in North and West Vancouver, Stanley Park and Garibaldi Park. At the same time, special effort was made to help the new Canadians among the children improve their spoken English, which greatly pleased their parents. This "impossible dream" continued every summer for a dozen years.

The new team members at First United Church in 1968 were immediately plunged into the busy summer program at Camp Fircom, and for the next seven years Glen Baker carried the

Leaders and staff enjoy the water at Camp Fircom.

leadership role for the Fircom Program Committee. His initiation came that first summer when he and his wife, Patricia, found themselves responsible for coordinating the week-long August family camp. Elsie Rosenberg directed a one-week camp for mothers and children, and Judy Langdon helped direct a ten-day camp for teen-aged girls. In the course of that summer all of the new staff members worked alongside a group of excellent volunteer camp directors to provide a truly positive camping experience for a total of four hundred children.

Fortunately for the ministers and community workers, the responsibility for the property and equipment was carried by the Camp Property Committee. Fircom, from its beginning in 1923, had been providing all the services of a small village, including electricity, water, and sewage, but the committee also had to organize the transportation of campers, leaders and supplies. Even after supplies reached the Fircom dock, they had to be transported up the steep hill to the dining hall. In the early years a horse, aptly named Old Dobbin, had hauled the heavy loads, but toward the end of the 1930s he was replaced by aged trucks.

Richmond Craig and student assistant Jack Crees with "Dobbin," the horse that hauled all the supplies up the steep hill at Camp Fircom on Gambier Island, northwest of Vancouver, from the mid-1920s until 1939.

Campfire Rock at Fircom in 1972.

While the new staff team members gallantly adapted to the rather primitive summer camp conditions at Fircom, back in the city there were greater challenges. Not only did clientele suffer from a bewildering array of personal difficulties and often spoke little or no English, but funding was chronically inadequate. In addition, staff members had to contend with worship services and worshippers, both of which could be described as unconventional. One Sunday evening in February 1971, in the middle of the live radio broadcast, the Reverend Glen Baker was making several announcements about church-related events when a good friend—one of the original Dugout volunteers—who was not entirely sober staggered up the aisle waving a piece of paper, which he handed to the preacher. It read: "Cut out the commercials and start preaching!" About a year later this same man learned that Mr. Baker was in hospital recovering from major surgery. He was anxious to pay the minister a visit in the hospital but was told that visitors were not permitted at that time. This didn't stop the resourceful man but only slowed him down a little. A few hours later he appeared at Glen's bedside, "freshly shaved and wearing a nifty suit which he had begged, borrowed, or otherwise acquired."[34] He had managed to convince all the authorities at the various checkpoints that he was a doctor!

First United was clearly in the business of dealing with local crises, although some of them originated far from the corner of Gore and Hastings. In August 1968 Russian tanks rolled into distant Prague to crush the uprising known as the "Prague Spring," driving thousands of despairing Czechs to flee their homeland. In the following months more than fourteen hundred Czech refugees arrived in Vancouver, placing impossible demands on the existing support systems. However, the new team member Linda Malila, who spoke fluent German (which was also spoken by many Czechs), had some understanding of the Czech language, so our team freed her up to work full-time with these new arrivals in our community. She became secretary of "Friends of Czechoslovakia," an organization set up to help the refugees find jobs and apartments. Another of her projects was the creation of a "Czech-In Centre" where immigrants could get information and make contact with Canadian families through educational and social programs. This involvement led to Linda chairing the Citizenship Council's Immigrant Services

Linda Malila, member of the staff from 1968 to 1971, provided strong community leadership in programs for new arrivals from Europe and Asia.

Committee, a volunteer group encouraged by the Citizenship Branch of the federal government to assist new immigrants with their registration and orientation to Canadian life.

From her involvement in this organization Linda learned that many immigrants from much earlier times were still unable to speak English. At the same time, Frank Fornelli, a summer student in the Inner-City Service Project, had been making that discovery in Vancouver's Italian community, where many of the women who had been in the city for as long as two decades had not learned to speak English. He helped to establish English classes for these women with an instructor who spoke Italian, and they dubbed the classes "School Italiana." A short time later the team at First United Church, the Pender YWCA and the Vancouver Inner-City Service Project joined forces to develop and expand it into "School Canadiana." All the classes were organized for members of single-language groups, each with a teacher who was familiar with that group's native language and culture. Childcare was also provided, something not available in traditional ESL courses at that time. Within a few months Linda was coordinating eight Japanese classes at First United, conducted by teachers who all spoke Japanese. There also were seven Chinese classes at the Pender YWCA and six Italian classes held in a Catholic Church in the Grandview area. Unfortunately for First United, Linda left in June 1971 to pursue a career teaching English as a second language in San Francisco.

Of course, no help was needed from totalitarian governments to maintain the steady supply of new problems for the First United team to address. Mercifully, however, many wonderfully capable people were drawn into the church's orbit to help deal with them, and collaborations with governments and other organizations also yielded some excellent results.

In the fall of 1969, First United Church was the venue for a week-long session of the federal government's Special Senate Committee on Poverty. Individuals and organizations were given the opportunity to present concerns to Senator David Croll's committee, and the general public was welcome to attend. On one of the hearing days a retired British army officer, recently arrived in Vancouver with his family, wandered into the church. He chatted in the corridor with one of our team members, showed an interest in what First United was doing and by the following week had been hired as part-time administrator of School Canadiana. His name was Peter Davies and he was to have a huge impact on the ministries of First United Church in the next few years.

Peter's natural community development skills were quickly recognized and appreciated by all members of the team, and within a few months we were able to find the funding to hire him as a community worker on a full-time basis. At our team

After Peter Davies died of Parkinson's disease on March 29, 2008, his daughter, Libby Davies, member of Parliament for Vancouver East since 1997, wrote these words for the "Lives Lived" column in the *Globe and Mail*:

It seems something of a contradiction that Peter Davies, a British soldier from age fourteen to his retirement as a major and arrival in Canada at age forty-one, became an activist for social justice for the last forty years of his life . . . Peter was always a radical and became well-known for his activism and passion for taking on injustice. He was a terrific organizer, maybe because of his old military precision and sense of order.

meetings, which provided a forum for frank discussion, he turned out to be a good listener, but he was also very persuasive and he always did his homework. A few weeks before his first meeting with us, Glen Baker had expressed his concern that many local people did not go to the hospitals or emergency clinics because they didn't have ready transportation or just felt uncomfortable away from their own community. He suggested that what we really needed was a health clinic in our neighbourhood. After Peter listened further to the team discussion on this topic, he said, "Why not?" Before long he was concentrating more than half of his time on the development of a downtown health clinic. As the project moved ahead, he contacted Dr. Donald Watt, director of United Church Health Services, to ask if the future clinic could be operated as part of the United Church network of mission hospitals. Dr. Watt explained that this was not possible, but he was able to provide a grant of $30,000 from the United Church's hospital discretionary account to help make the clinic a reality.

Space was secured in the 300 block of East Cordova Street, Dr. Kes Chetty became the medical director and a support staff was assembled. Peter continued to work closely with the new clinic, and at one of our team meetings he expressed the need for a dental clinic as part of this new project. The following week, after I had attended Church Union meetings in Ontario and while chatting with the friend driving me back to the Toronto airport, I learned that my friend's brother-in-law, Dr. Ron Martin of Owen Sound, Ontario, had recently taken early retirement from his dental practice. My friend passed on the word about our need for a dentist, and the following week Ron flew out to meet with the clinic staff and the board; a few weeks later, he and his wife Mary became part of the First United Church community. Using his network of dental friends across the country, Ron obtained, at no cost, all the equipment necessary for the clinic, installed it himself, and began operating a very busy dental clinic as part of the Downtown Community Health Society. When his six-month locum was completed, a permanent dentist was hired to take his place.

Another new project was initiated in the summer of 1969 by David Hembling, a theological student who was part of the Vancouver Inner-City Service Project. The Vancouver Crisis Intervention and Suicide Prevention Centre that he organized brought together psychiatrist Dr. Paul Termansen, the Reverend Glen Baker, lawyer Jon Jessiman, social worker Ben Chud, nurse Betty Tarrant and several other community members. These founders believed that a listening service could help people in distress and that a crisis centre would provide a place to turn for those in pain. Similar centres had been organized in many North American cities. Many Vancouver community leaders knew such a centre was needed, but it took one passionate student to bring the necessary professionals together around this important project. By the end of 1969 the Crisis Centre was registered and operating in the medical-dental building at Broadway and Burrard. The first year's budget was $30,000, with only one staff person supported by many volunteers to maintain a round-the-clock service.

In that same summer of 1969. the men's work program at First United moved in a new direction with the help of Joe Cannon, a new member of our staff. Joe had been an organizer for the Canadian Brotherhood of Railway Employees for much of his career and had also been one of the first members of Alcoholics Anonymous when it was introduced to Vancouver twenty-five years earlier. Although seventy-four years old when he joined our staff, he was on duty each morning for the next six years, referring people to the daily AA meeting at the Dugout, a few blocks from the church, or giving helpful, practical advice to the men who came to see him. He helped hundreds of men to get started on the road to sobriety, and his down-to-earth counselling set a very high standard for all who followed him in later years.

Every few years the Board of Home Missions, which generously funded institutional churches like First United in cities across Canada, encouraged or initiated a review of the work of its missions, always searching for more efficient and effective ways to fulfill their purpose. In 1968 Dr. H.A. (Jamie) Wallin, a professor in the Faculty of Education at UBC, had been engaged to review all the United Church outreach work in the Lower Mainland, which included all of the area from Hope to the Sunshine Coast. This study was financed with a grant from the Vancouver Foundation. One of the outcomes of his review was the establishment of the Metropolitan Council of the Lower Mainland, with representation from each of the four presbyteries of Fraser, Westminster, Vancouver South and Vancouver Burrard. This council was given two full-time clergy staff members—the Reverend Gordon Laird, who had been a chartered accountant before becoming an ordained minister in 1968, and the Reverend Jack Shaver, who had been the United Church chaplain at UBC for ten years, was a theologian and had a passion for social justice. They shared

The reverends Jack Shaver and Gordon Laird were appointed to the staff of the Metropolitan Council when it was formed in 1969.

a single job description: either singly or together, to research, plan and administer oversight of all non-congregational ministries and projects of the church in the Lower Mainland. For First United, the establishment of the Metropolitan Council meant the removal of some of the responsibilities formerly carried by the superintendent—for example, overseeing the ethnic ministries—but the two new clergy provided fresh advice, encouragement and support at regular meetings with the team.

This support became especially important in 1970 when thousands of young people converged on Vancouver. Since the mid-1960s the Vancouver Cool-Aid Society, organized by young people to help other transient young people, had been operating two hostels in the city, and by 1969, the first year that Cool-Aid received some token civic financial support, it was providing housing for more than fifty teenagers each night. But the Cool-Aid premises were constantly being raided by police drug squads and the organizers' work was regularly hampered by bylaw enforcement officers, so that, according to journalist Denny Boyd, the society was clinging "to a precarious life, succeeding marginally in spite of the Establishment."[35] As a result, when an especially large number of transient youth hit the city in the summer of 1970, Cool-Aid couldn't cope, and the young people began camping out at Jericho Beach in the long-unused seaplane and flying boat hangars built for the air force in World War II. They were evicted in mid-September, and First

United agreed to use its gymnasium as a dormitory for fifty of the young men while the downtown YWCA provided space for fifty young women. In collaboration with the Inner-City Service Project and the Vancouver Cool-Aid Society, First United also provided meals for three hundred each day through a "Feed-In" program at Kitsilano Beach. The food was donated by farmers in the Lower Mainland, community merchants and churches, and it was prepared by volunteers who worked in the church kitchen each day. To transport the food from First United to the beach, we used the old, full-sized bus that Cool-Aid had acquired to carry people and supplies to the various places where youth gathered around the city. To secure insurance for the bus,

Transient youth on Jericho Beach in Vancouver line up for food served to them by Cool-Aid, the Inner-City Service Project and First United Church, in 1970. The meals were all prepared by volunteers in the First United kitchen.

I purchased it from Cool-Aid for a dollar and became its registered owner for one year. In these new projects we were guided and fully supported by Gordon Laird and Jack Shaver of the Metropolitan Council, both of whom had been closely involved with the Vancouver Inner-City Service Project in previous years, so they were not thrown off balance by the counter-culture atmosphere at the "Feed-In" or in the church gym. Because we had to respond quickly to emergency situations, the support of these two men also made us feel more confident.

In the early 1970s the federal government began making Local Initiatives Project (LIP) grants available to provide employment

---

In October 1971 the members of the First United Church Team prepared the following statement of their commitment to working with other organizations:

COOPERATIVE PROGRAMS AND PROJECTS

We believe we should never "go it alone" on a program in our community unless all efforts to work with other churches and agencies have failed. Increasingly the staff members are involved in programs outside the First United building. We see our church as a catalyst in the community, helping to spark new responses to community needs and problems . . . Through the Strathcona Area Services Team we share in overall planning for programs in the entire community, making our building and staff members available where possible. We are closely involved with or share in the leadership of McLean Park Nursery School, the Dugout Day Centre, the Downtown Community Health Society, the Crisis Centre, the Inner-City Service Project, the Downtown-Eastside Clergy Association, the Opportunity Rehabilitation Workshop (formerly Welfare Industries of First United Church), Meals-on-Wheels for Strathcona and downtown areas, the Strathcona Summer Enrichment Program, YWCA and Parks Board Recreation programs and programs for teens in Strathcona. Most of these take place outside our building but our staff members take an active part in them. These are in addition to the community programs held in our church and to which all interested people in the community are invited: Happy Hours (our weekly program for seniors), Saturday Night Fellowship (for downtown men), Hockey Night (our weekly supper for fifty men while we watch the Canucks Hockey Telecast), Scouts, Cubs, and a Community Girls Group.

in community service projects, and First United Church was successful in securing one of them for a program to relate to young people living on the streets. The project's primary aim was to provide liaison between young Native people and the other people in their lives, including social workers. The thirty-one-year-old director we hired for this outreach project, Hugh Jordan, was able to report in December 1973 that "we've had contact with about three hundred kids since we started—in any one week the figure would be about seventy-five to a hundred."[36] This project eventually led to the conversion of a portion of the upstairs Sunday school area of the church into a classroom for an outreach school for twenty-five to thirty teenaged high school dropouts. The Vancouver School Board arranged for this school to be administered by Britannia Secondary and, recognizing its importance, funded it for the next twenty-five years.

At First United we had long known that many unemployed people, far from enjoying their lives of dependency, desperately wanted to find jobs but had difficulty presenting themselves to prospective employers. To combat this problem, we teamed up with Canada Manpower for a six-month experiment between October 1973 and March 1974 to establish a Basic Job Readiness Training program that would help people assess and upgrade their skills. At any one time there were up to forty students at the church, ranging in age from the late teens to almost retirement age. Each received $55 per week and participated in an eight-week intensive self-assessment course for job hunters. Statistics are not available for this program, but we believe about one-third of the people who completed the course were successful in finding employment. This project was not renewed after the six-month period ended.

In 1972 Maurice Egan, the city of Vancouver's director of social planning, approached us with a proposal that eventually led to many changes in our community. The city wanted to hire Peter

Davies as a social planner for the downtown community but have him located in an office at First United Church rather than City Hall. First United agreed to this arrangement, and Peter's first assignment in his new role was to co-ordinate an LIP grant program that had been submitted before he began his work with the city. This program, known as "People's Aid," employed ten people who were sent to work at several community agencies where they were to look for gaps in services. Among the workers hired in this project were Bill Hennessy, Lawrence Bantleman and Bruce Erikson, all of whom would contribute generously to the community in the years that followed.

Over the period from the late 1960s to the early 1970s, First United Church's social action mission loomed so large that it is easy to forget that this church was also just what its name implies—a United Church congregation. In fact, while the mission work was constantly expanding, the congregation was steadily shrinking. During the Craig and Roddan eras Sunday morning attendance had typically been about four hundred and evening

Following his participation in the People's Aid Project, Bruce Erikson became a public figure in Vancouver. He was born in Winnipeg in 1928, and after a difficult childhood there, left home at fourteen to ride the freight trains to the West Coast. He found jobs in the logging industry on Vancouver Island, worked in a shipyard in Vancouver during World War II and was a member of the Seafarers' International Union of Canada before becoming an ironworker.

In 1973, along with Jean Swanson and Libby Davies, Bruce founded the Downtown Eastside Residents' Association (DERA) to provide a democratic organization for residents of the area. DERA pressured the city government to pass a bylaw requiring hotels to have sprinkler systems to reduce the number of area deaths by fire. DERA also pressured the city to create the Carnegie Community Centre. In 1980 Bruce won his first election to Vancouver City Council and served as a councillor for the next twelve years. His contribution to improving the lives of citizens in the Downtown Eastside was enormous. He died in March 1997 after a one-year battle with cancer.

The First United Church congregation held an Easter Service at Sunset Beach in April 1972, complete with helium-filled balloons.

attendance as much as a thousand. By the late 1960s morning attendance was sixty or seventy with thirty or forty persons normally attending the evening radio service. However, support for the mission was coming from United Church congregations all over the Lower Mainland, although the vast majority of the mission's supporters worshipped in their home churches.

This is not to say that the First United's small congregation was moribund. There were still many members who had been actively involved for forty years or more. There was also a lively program, coordinated by Al and Peggy Peterson, in which the children from the Sunday school community shared a creative and exciting few years with the children from the Finnish language congregation that worshipped in the chapel each Sunday and a dozen children from staff families. They got rid of excess energy by bouncing on the inflated inner tube salvaged from a huge truck, then formed small groups where they created ways to act out the scripture lesson for the day. For many children and families, Sunday morning at First United remained a great adventure.

JACK SHAVER, 1973–1982

In July 1973 a new member joined the staff team at First United Church whose intense personality and extraordinary gifts had an effect on the entire institution. Jack Shaver added great theological and pastoral insight to all dimensions of the work. He also related with surprising effectiveness to many of the men and women in the community, though surprising only because he was so well known for his deep theological conversations. He was a lover of words and in worship or in conversation was often able to say just the right thing to bring challenge, comfort or laughter. At one of the Sunday morning services he spoke this prayer:

Jack Shaver had been raised in a Winnipeg manse during the years that his father served an inner-city mission. Such an upbringing could leave many boys resentfully yearning for a comfortable bourgeois life; it left Jack with a unique mixture of compassion and respect for the hurting, lonely people at the margins of our communities. After ordination in the United Church, he served in pastoral ministries for fifteen years before becoming the United Church campus chaplain at UBC in 1959. After a decade of outstanding service during turbulent times on the campus, Jack joined the Metropolitan Council staff and then in 1973 brought his ministry gifts to First United Church.

Our Father, we bring our personal cares and common needs before you. Even though we come together we come trying, each one to bring the concerns of each other one.

We are all scared. There are some here who are really scared, in some deep dread or terror they can't name. Empower them to grasp life anyway. It's a gift to be able to grasp what terrifies us instead of fleeing it. Your gift.

We are all enslaved, but there are some who are more enslaved. Hear their cry. It's a gift to be liberated. Your gift.

We all hurt, but there are those who really hurt. Their pain is overwhelming. Hear their cry. Buoy them up. May they find you, your gift of yourself entering into all human pain and sorrow.

We are all lonely. Some are really lonely. We are your gift to one another. Work that giving and receiving in our midst this morning.

We are all weary. Who is more weary than any other? This world of ours has got to us. We are not up to it unless we are constantly restored. The world has really got to us. Just any old restoration is not enough. Nothing short of your restoration is sufficient.

From 1973 until his retirement in 1982, Jack was a huge blessing for the staff team, the congregation and the Downtown Eastside community. In an essay written six months after he became a member of the First United team, he talked about working in the inner city:

In a way, the inner city is like a small town. Everything is within walking distance. A lot of the people you meet know all the same people. Many of the inhabitants never venture far beyond the area.

In another way it is very different. You are overwhelmed by the number whose lonely suffering goes unnoticed. You face a constant stream of what we would call the lost, the hurting, the beat, the dispossessed, the deviant. Too many of the inhabitants are on a one-way trip to destruction. Too high an incidence of violence and crime are concentrated here.

There is no adequate accounting for the inner city's fascination. For many it is a chosen environment. Most of its inhabitants would come right back if they were transplanted. This is where they have worked out their response to the challenges and defeats of life. This is where they have culminated a long history of making out. It's home.

Caring people (if that is who make up the church), when they get the feel of the inner city, can't help but ache that something be done. The church faces an enormous challenge in discovering what it is called to do . . . But the central concern of the church is that a ministry be accountable to the people served. Take a program aimed at befriending street kids. Most of them have at least one worker with some kind of authority over them like police, probation officer, social worker or the Children's Aid. They have chosen to live on the streets rather than comply, and some of them have been doing this since the age of nine or ten.

A street worker who is dedicated to befriending these kids, to operating with a deep awareness of what it is like to be the clients of these official programs, cannot help but be suspected by the agencies of aiding and abetting this anti-social behaviour.

At the same time, the kids' choice for the street is almost

certainly a choice for destruction. The street worker who completely identifies with the kids, who responds to their wants only, contributes to this destruction. Yet to dream about alternative lifestyles for these kids risks offending them and is almost indistinguishable from putting them down.[37]

First United was also blessed with the services of many other talented people during these years, some for short-term projects and others for a year or two. These included Mary Bastedo, Kathryn Anderson, Mary Cayley, Gail Price, Dode Stansfield, Jim Stimson and Vicki Obedkoff. We were also blessed with many fine support staff members whose faithful services made everything else possible. That long list would include Pat Clarke, Erma Francis, Joan Birchall, Marg Maxwell, Eleanor Jackson, Ann Farrell, Jennie Jones, Babe Diwell, Jack Mitchell and Bill Foster.

Visiting the members of the congregation and community in their homes or in hospital was a special assignment usually carried by a retired minister. From 1968 to 1972 the Reverend Reg Redman was our pastoral visitor, and he was succeeded by the Reverend Roy Stobie, who was with us for several years as pastoral visitor and wise counsellor almost fifty years after he had become a member of First United. Both he and the Reverend Redman used their long history with First United and their genuine interest in people to great advantage. In 1974 this responsibility was given to the Reverend Ray Tingley, a Baptist minister recently retired from the Bible Society office. For the next ten years, Ray made visits to hundreds of radio listeners, present and former members of the congregation and other friends of First United Church. For at least fifteen years, coordinating those requesting visits and corresponding with them was the volunteer work of B. Louise Foster, a retired overseas missionary.

Through the gifts that each of these people brought to First United Church, we were able to extend the range of programs and services within the community and assist in the development of community-based organizations. By the mid-1970s First United had become an important part of a network of churches and community agencies committed to constructive social action. We had inherited a new building and remarkable goodwill for which thanks must go to those who preceded us. Our building space, staff energy and, occasionally, financial resources had helped to establish significant new programs.

In July 1974 I left First United Church to become a full-time member of the newly created British Columbia Police Commission. I had no experience in policing work but had been serving on the Vancouver Police Commission for a year, although this had been a part-time involvement with only monthly meetings and the occasional additional responsibility. Now the provincial government had decided to create a police commission to coordinate all policing policy, training and citizen complaint procedures. They decided to have three commissioners, one of whom would be from the community, and that was to be my post. The other two commissioners were a former deputy commissioner of the RCMP and a lawyer with a doctorate in criminology. I was assigned lead responsibility for the relationship the police had with social services, Native people, women and minority groups.

The Reverend Glen Baker was appointed acting superintendent of First United Church for the following year, and most of the team members continued in their positions during that year. The Reverend Jack Shaver shared the preaching and pastoral responsibilities and provided continuity in the next part of this story. Glen Baker left in July 1975 to become the minister at Dunbar Heights United Church in Vancouver.

═CHAPTER 6═

1975–1987

Art Griffin, Superintendent, 1975–1980

The Reverend Art Griffin began his ministry as superintendent of First United Church on November 1, 1975. He shared the leadership of the Sunday morning and evening worship services with the Reverend Jack Shaver, and they both participated in the twenty-minute magazine portion of the radio broadcast, an innovation that had been introduced in 1972 by reducing the original hour-long worship portion to forty minutes. This new section, which covered news and interviews on church-related topics, was coordinated by the Reverend Rod Booth, the BC Conference's broadcasting minister, who gathered material for the show by interviewing First United staff members and other people of interest to the church community. When Art Griffin arrived in 1975, he was enthusiastic about the magazine component of the broadcast, and each year at the annual meeting of the BC Conference he would move through the six hundred delegates with his trusty tape recorder in hand, interviewing delegates who had interesting stories to tell. Later he would edit the

Arthur Griffin was born in Winnipeg in 1921. As a youth he was passionate about music, activities in the church and playing cricket. By 1939, the year that the national junior cricket tournament was being held in Vancouver, he had joined the Manitoba Junior Cricket Team. Both of Art's parents travelled to Vancouver with him that June and attended the games in which he played, and then they helped him look for a place to live. He found room and board for $4 a week in a lovely home in Kitsilano, three blocks from the ocean. He was happy to leave behind Winnipeg's "extreme cold, extreme heat, violent thunderstorms, swarms of mosquitoes, and countless dragonflies."[38]

After five months of applying for jobs all over the city, Art was hired as a delivery boy and shelf stacker in a grocery store at $7 per week. After six months he was invited to work at the Lewis Piano Company, still at $7 per week, cleaning out pianos, steelwooling piano strings and filing action hammers, but the job did allow him Wednesdays and Saturday afternoons off to play cricket. A few months later he moved to the Kelly Piano Company where he became a piano restorer and cleaner but also learned how to tune pianos. In 1942 he joined the RCAF where he trained as a mechanic. After being posted to Claresholm, Alberta, then to Calgary, he again became involved in young people's church activities and serious cricket matches. He also became good friends with the Air Force chaplain and helped out by playing the piano for worship services.

When he was discharged at Jericho Beach RCAF Station in Vancouver late in the summer of 1945, he had a clear career goal in mind: he would become a United Church minister. He immediately began taking the matriculation courses he would need to attend UBC and ultimately achieve ordained ministry. He met Pearl Leggett a year later and they were married on June 13, 1947. For the next fifty years they were a true team, sharing in ministry together. In addition to all the contributions Pearl made to the local congregations where Art was ministering, she also served a term as national president of United Church Women and for almost a year was the acting executive secretary of the BC Conference.

After his ordination in 1951, Art served in several congregations. They included Port Kells United, Surrey, 1951–54; Failsworth, England, 1954–55; Cedar Cottage United, Vancouver, 1955–1960; Trinity United, Port Coquitlam, 1960–66; St. Stephen's United, Edmonton, 1966–1970; and Brechin United, Nanaimo, 1970–75.

tapes and, with the help of Rod Booth, share the stories with the Sunday evening radio listeners.

From the earliest years of his ministry Art had been actively concerned about social justice issues. While serving at St. Stephen's United Church in Edmonton in the late 1960s, he was

The Reverend Art Griffin, who was superintendent from 1975 to 1980.

given the opportunity to participate in the six-week Canadian Urban Training (CUT) program in Toronto. He found this course both challenging and encouraging, but he was especially in tune with the program's emphasis on proactively seeking more adequate government support for low-income individuals and families. At First United Church he was able to fully apply his energy to organizing coalitions on behalf of the poor that would challenge those in power to deal more compassionately with the hurting members of the community.

Art wrote many letters to public officials, sometimes on behalf of a coalition of churches and agencies, sometimes on behalf of First United and sometimes just because he was frustrated or angry at the apparent indifference of public officials to the plight of people in the community. He also wrote countless letters to the editors of local newspapers, raising issues about which he was passionate. Although there was little evidence that these letters accomplished the requested change of mind or policy, Art was relentless in pursuing this strategy. Occasionally he got replies to his letters that only added to his anger and frustration. For example, when a new remand centre was being planned for a location adjacent to the Main Street police station, the members of the Downtown-Eastside Clergy Association registered their opposition by having Art write a letter. The government response was clear and unequivocal; the project would proceed as planned.

But there were times when the responses Art received to his protests made him cheer. He frequently spoke out at meetings of the city council when he was opposed to a decision that had been made or one that appeared likely. When he learned that the councillors were planning to vote six to five against a request by the Downtown Eastside Residents' Association (DERA) to fund three staff positions, he appeared at the next council meeting to speak on DERA's behalf. He offered the goodwill and services of First United Church to organize and administer the grant for DERA, and the funding was approved eight votes to three. It

Jennie Jones with Art Griffin, who is honouring Jennie's service as the resident hostess at First United Church for eleven years.

was a small victory but a good reminder that politicians are impressed when they see agencies and churches working together. In using First United Church as a platform from which he could challenge the authorities, Art felt he was following in the steps of both the Old Testament prophets and Andrew Roddan, who had led the work at First United Church during the Depression years.

Art also sought to continue the emphasis on team ministry. Elsie Rosenberg, Jack Shaver and Bill Hennessy had been part of the team when he arrived. A year later Elsie left the staff to be minister of a church in Powell River, BC, but her departure was balanced by the arrival on staff of diaconal minister Linda Ervin. Long-time volunteer Babe Diwell assumed part-time staff responsibilities at this time, and Beth Jennings, Dorothy Manson and Goldvine Howard joined the team.

Art and Pearl Griffin chose to make Happy Hours a high priority for their time and energy. This was the Wednesday afternoon program that had been started in the mid-1950s to provide a weekly social and program afternoon for seniors associated with the congregation or other community programs. Art and Pearl also participated regularly in the Saturday Night Fellowship, another weekly program that had been functioning for twenty-seven years. Both of these programs provided the opportunity to mingle with members of the community and get to know them by name. Members of these groups appreciated Art's piano contributions from time to time.

Bill Hennessy had become

Dorothy Manson worked in the office from the late 1970s to the mid-1980s.

a member of the staff team in March 1973, following his participation in the six-month-long People's Aid Program. He had twenty-five years of experience as a counsellor with the Royal Canadian Legion and the Department of Veterans Affairs. While working on the People's Aid Project, Bill had discovered that large numbers of men and women in the First United community were not receiving the benefits to which they were entitled, and within a period of six months he personally assisted thirty downtown residents to apply for and receive those benefits. After he joined the First United team, the words "advocate" and "advocacy" became part of the new program language. He served as an advocate for hundreds of men and women who had been unjustly denied benefits from the health, welfare or social housing systems. Bill also helped to encourage and train other advocates, laying the foundation for the advocacy program that has been at the centre of First United's ministry ever since. He was especially supportive of those who lived in terrible housing conditions, those who were handicapped, and war veterans who did not receive appropriate levels of support.

In 1976, along with staff members Joan Birchall, Babe Diwell and Elsie Rosenburg, Bill was instrumental in establishing the Downtown Handicapped Association (DHA), whose main emphasis was to serve the needs of the disabled. The program was set up so that it could be run by its members, and soon up to forty members were meeting two afternoons each week. Programs consisted of games, crafts, conversation, singing, dancing, movies and refreshments. In 1979 the DHA was incorporated as a society, and in 1981 a "handicapped camp" evolved for those disabled people who were part of the First United community. Camp Squamish, run by the Lions Club, became available and with the help of the Lions Club and an initial grant from the United Way, a new camping adventure was under way. Beth Jennings, who was on the program staff at First United, spearheaded this

On May 29, 2001, the fiftieth anniversary of Art Griffin's ordination, at a regular meeting of the Vancouver Burrard Presbytery, the presbytery gave a tribute to him, as recorded in the presbytery minutes:

The following citation was presented by Marilyn Harrison, former BC Conference archivist and long-time friend of the Griffins. She described Art as "something like a Yorkshire Terrier—small, wiry and free-spirited; combative, courageous, and willing to take on anyone and anything; persistent in not letting go once its teeth are into something; noisy in making itself heard when it is upset or disturbed; impulsive; friendly; loyal and fun-loving to be with when it likes you." Marilyn went on to identify common threads that ran throughout his ministry and were certainly significant in his work at First United Church:

- fighting for justice on behalf of the voiceless ones from a biblical base
- his love of music and sports, especially cricket and curling
- having fun with, being supportive of, and being supported by the family
- having the companionship, love and support of Pearl whose calming influence was key for this aggressive, combative, persistent, impulsive, fun-loving and free-spirited fellow.[39]

program until 1987, relying heavily on her accordion and her love for people to make each meeting special.

After he resigned from his position at the church in June 1980 for health reasons and moved to the South Okanagan area, Bill was certainly missed.

In 1979 changes occurring at a higher organizational level of the United Church would ultimately influence the way the First United mission was governed. The changes began when the Metropolitan Council, created in 1969 to have oversight of all the outreach and institutional work in the Lower Mainland, was dissolved in 1979, its responsibilities assigned to other conference or presbytery committees. The Oversight Committee, created by the council in 1976 to have full responsibility for the First United Church ministry, and which had for three years reported directly to the Metropolitan Council, now began reporting to the Vancouver Burrard Presbytery. Fortunately, this Oversight Committee, which would become known as the Oversight Board in the late 1980s, was composed of representatives from various community and professional backgrounds and they still met regularly to guide the direction of the mission. Their guidance became very important later that year.

During Art Griffin's years at First United, one of his most difficult challenges was his relationship with Camp Fircom. Most of the members of the Camp Fircom Committee were men and women who had been campers, leaders or summer staff members in recent years. Their commitment to the campers and their families was impressive, but their understanding of how to express the Christian or spiritual aspects of the camp program was very different from the more traditional philosophy of Christian camping that had always been an important part of Art's ministry, a philosophy to which he was still firmly committed. As a consequence, a crisis arose in 1979, and the Camp Fircom Committee, with the support of First United Church Oversight Committee, incorporated as a society; the camp was no longer a program arm of First United Church. This was a huge disappointment for Art, who felt that he was not being supported by the Oversight Committee in a vital aspect of his ministry. In January 1980 he made the decision to resign, effective June 30. He was subsequently called to St. Andrew's United Church in Mission, BC, and began his ministry there in July.

John Cashore, Superintendent, 1980–1986

In July 1980 Art Griffin was succeeded as superintendent at First United by the Reverend John Cashore. The new superintendent was very familiar with the First United church building, the community surrounding the church and the general nature of the special challenges he would face there because, back in the early seventies when he had served as the Native Affairs Consultant for the BC Conference of the United Church, his office had been located within First United Church. He brought to his new assignment his passion for social justice and his great respect for First Nations people and their culture. Reflecting on the situation that faced him when he arrived in 1980, John Cashore wrote:

> The agenda for the people in the Downtown Eastside was decided by the plans for BC Place and Expo '86. Introduced by Premier Bennett with the economy still riding a boom, the massive two hundred-acre development on the north shore of False Creek was to be the largest urban redevelopment in the history of North America.[40]

This urban redevelopment, however, promised to wipe out the living accommodations of large numbers of the elderly, the poor, the unemployed and the handicapped. The team at First United Church decided to address the urgent need for social housing and contracted with Larry Bantleman to do a study of the housing

The Reverend John Cashore, who was superintendent from 1980 to 1986.

John Cashore was born in March 1935 in Lethbridge. His father died when he was just two years old and his mother, a registered nurse, worked twelve-hour days to raise him and his two older sisters alone. John recalls how important Southminster United Church was for his family, and largely because of the warm support of the people in the congregation, he was very young when he began to think seriously about becoming a minister. He worked part-time during high school at a local dairy and during the summer of 1951 on a survey crew to earn money for university. After earning his BA at UBC in 1958, he took his first-year theological studies at Union College. In 1959–60 he worked for First United Church in Prince Rupert where he was strongly influenced by teamwork with the Reverend Dr. Bob Elliot, who was also the founder of Prince Rupert's Friendship House, an outreach mission working with First Nations people. John returned to Union College and married Sharon in December 1961, then was ordained in May 1962 and posted to the First Nations community of Lax Kw'alaams, then known as Port Simpson, twenty-five miles north of Prince Rupert.

After four years at Lax Kw'alaams, John Cashore served as minister at East Trail United Church for three years. In 1969 he was appointed Native Affairs Consultant for the BC Conference. (It was only recently that he learned that his own mother's grandmother, Annie Lazotte, had been Metis; his mother's family had its roots in the Red River Settlement.) After four years as a consultant, he was called to Queens Avenue United Church in New Westminster where he worked in a team ministry for five years with the Reverend Charles Raymont.

crisis in the area surrounding the church and make appropriate recommendations for action. During the years when Larry had been on the board of the Downtown Eastside Residents' Association, from 1973 to 1981, the association had been monitoring single-room occupancy in that area and keeping lists of hotels and rooming houses that were in violation of health and safety codes. At the same time the City of Vancouver's Social Planning Department had been developing the numbers essential to support the case for creating more social housing in the community. Larry's job, therefore, was to collate these reports, along with all the statistics he could pull from the most recent census and from other community studies, and then to add the technical expertise of Joe Wai and Ron Yuen, a team of architects who had amassed a deep knowledge of the community's housing needs. He turned in his report in June 1981. The report concluded with a recommendation that First United create a social housing society and move forward in consultation with the Canada Mortgage and Housing Corporation (CMHC), the City of Vancouver and the BC Housing Corporation to create social housing either on the corner of Gore and Hastings—the site of First United—or on land nearby.

Within a month the First United Church Social Housing Society was formed, a society that would, over the next several years, require major time commitments from all First United church staff members. In July the CMHC approved the first funding phase, and on August 4, 1981, the society held its first meeting, chaired by Linda Ervin, the diaconal minister who had been working as an advocate since 1976 and who was convinced of the urgent need to provide additional social housing. The new society was supported by a strong volunteer board, elected at the first meeting of the society, but a project so large was a huge responsibility for any group of volunteers to undertake. They were fortunate to have the support of Art Jones, the administrator of the BC Conference of the United Church. He guided the society's treasurer and executive through many challenging situations. As well, they had the expertise of Larry Bantleman as a consultant, who helped to prepare the board members for the many discussions with city, provincial and federal officials. Henri Lock, a volunteer board member, secretary of the society from 1982 to 1984 and board chair from 1984 to 1986, contributed substantially to the project's success, providing leadership in negotiations with city, provincial and CMHC officials. Passionate about the need for social housing, he made himself available almost daily for months at a time, even though he had other heavy commitments. He was a student at the Vancouver School of Theology, but from 1982 to 1984 worked as a childcare worker

Larry Bantleman was born in 1942 in the city of Bangalore in southern India, five years before the partition of British India into Pakistan, Bangladesh and India. In a reflection in the February 1983 issue of the church's newsletter *First Things First*, he wrote:

> The year was 1948 and we were living in Bangalore, South India. Dreadful communal/religious violence had broken out in Bengal and the Punjab, the two provinces most affected by Partition . . . We were Christians in Hindu/Muslim India. I was six years old. I remember that evening [January 30, 1948] as we gathered around the wireless to hear of the news of Gandhi's assassination in Birla House in New Delhi.[41]

Larry was in his early twenties when he came to Canada. In 1972 he was hired by Peter Davies as one of the staff for the six-month-long People's Aid program based at First United Church. When the project ended in the spring of 1973, he became the founder and editor of a weekly newspaper for the Downtown Eastside and then a member of the staff and board of the Downtown Eastside Residents' Association. He was committed to the cause of better housing and living conditions in the Downtown Eastside and he was soon well respected by the Canada Mortgage and Housing Corporation as well as public servants in the civic government offices.

at The Maples, an adolescent treatment centre in Burnaby, before returning to the School of Theology to complete his degree.

After nine months of detailed discussions with architects, city planners and CMHC officials, it became clear that it was not financially viable to tear down the existing church and build both a new church and affordable housing on the property at Gore and Hastings. CMHC was prepared to loan funds for the housing but not for the replacement of the church as well. Since the numbers simply did not work on that site, the society began the search for suitable property in the surrounding community.

Finally, in 1983 a site at Jackson and Hastings owned by the City of Vancouver was selected, for which the society negotiated a forty-one-year lease. Architects Joe Wai and Ron Yuen joined forces to design the first housing project, and Van Maren Construction was hired to build it. After further financial negotiations with government agencies, in the summer of 1984, right on schedule, the first of the society's social housing projects became a reality. The seven-storey building was named Bill Hennessy Place in honour of the man who had been an advocate at First United from 1973 to 1980 and who had helped hundreds of men and women to gain the benefits to which they were entitled. It opened with seventy units: twenty-four bachelor, thirty-one one-bedroom and fifteen two-bedroom apartments. A second building, eight storeys high and designed and built by the same team, was constructed across the street on the south side of Hastings and opened in 1987. Named Jennie Pentland Place in honour of the tireless women's worker on the staff of First United from 1923 until 1936, it has eighty-six units: forty-four bachelor, twenty-five one-bedroom, eleven two-bedroom and six three-bedroom apartments.

Even before this second building was completed, a third First United Church Social Housing Society project was under way at the special request of CMHC and the City of Vancouver.[42] Ledingham Place in the community of Mount Pleasant was planned for those families that had a member living with physical handicaps requiring modified interiors, including appliances and furnishings. Many new challenges arose with this project, because the large heritage home of the Ledingham family had to be restored and retained within the development. The development also had to be named after the family. This project opened in 1989 with thirteen one-bedroom, fourteen two-bedroom and six three-bedroom apartments.

During the decade that the housing projects were being planned and constructed, other programs at First United were undergoing significant developments. The handicapped program led by

Beth Jennings made great use of her accordion as a program worker from 1981 to 1987.

Beth Jennings was supported by increasing numbers of volunteers who had made this program a priority. Many men and women who lived near the church discovered that they were welcomed as volunteers, and they were invited to be part of a "mission assist team" that provided training and attempted to match personal gifts with needs.

In 1980 another new initiative, a literacy program, was organized in cooperation with the King Edward Campus of Vancouver Community College. Hundreds of men and women of all ages participated in this opportunity, four afternoons per week, to learn basic literacy skills. A room in First United, formerly known as the South Hall, served as the literacy classroom. This program continues to serve the Downtown Eastside community in 2010.

The advocacy position left vacant when Bill Hennessy retired from the staff in 1980 was filled by Alan Alvare, a former Roman Catholic priest. He and the diaconal minister Linda Ervin were joined in 1981 by Leslie Black, and all three were designated "community workers." They divided their time between one-on-one advocacy, helping individuals, and social advocacy, addressing those systemic issues that caused serious problems for individuals.

In 1981 Bob Stewart became a part-time member of the First Church team when he moved into the apartment at First United Church. A graduate of UBC and the Vancouver School of Theology (MDiv), Bob was the archivist for the BC Conference of the United Church from 1980 until his death in November

2005. It was a half-time salaried position, although Bob worked close to full time. From 1981 to 1994 he was the host of the Saturday Night Fellowship, the church's weekend custodian, an active member of the First United board and congregation and the founding editor of the church newsletter, *First Things First*. In 1983 he began researching the history of First United, hoping to write and publish it during the church's centennial year, 1985, but was unable to accomplish this self-imposed assignment. However, some of his notes and the scripts for presentations he made to church groups about First United's history have been very helpful in shaping parts of this book.

The same year that Bob Stewart arrived at First United, Jim Hatherly worked out of the church on a six-month experimental "street ministry." A recent graduate of the Vancouver School of Theology, Jim functioned as a "detached worker" by visiting the bars, restaurants and streets of the Downtown Eastside frequented by juvenile and adult prostitutes and communicating with them there. He found there was considerable interest in the support of First United in the nearby area, but less appreciation when he extended his work to the Granville and Davie areas. His final report was welcomed by the Oversight Committee as its contents helped to prepare the members for future decisions on the church's mission to sex-trade workers.

The congregation at First United Church showed great courage in 1981 when Tim Stevenson, an openly gay man studying at the Vancouver

Bob Stewart, BC Conference Archivist, was resident host and part-time staff member of First United Church from 1981 to 1994.

School of Theology, became a member of the congregation and asked to be sponsored as a candidate for ordained ministry. He became an intended candidate in 1982 and for most of the next decade was a member of the congregational board. He participated in the committee process at the 1988 General Council meeting in Victoria where the council made the decision that sexual orientation was not a barrier to ordained ministry in the United Church. Four years later, in 1992, Tim became the first openly gay person to be ordained in the United Church of Canada.

Following the retirement of Jack Shaver in 1982, the Reverend Barry Morris was called to be the minister of the congregation. His primary responsibility was to serve the congregation, though whenever possible he involved John Cashore and other staff members in the Sunday services. At the same time, however, Barry also developed a ministry to people on the street, relating to men and women in cafes and drop-in centres, on the street corners and in the Carnegie Centre. Sometimes in the late evenings, accompanied by women from the congregation, he would take coffee to sex-trade workers on the street corners. He was available at all hours to all people who might need his encouragement, friendship or support, and in so doing he soon created a street presence that added a new dimension to the church's relationship to the community. But Barry was also interested in all the other aspects of

The Reverend Barry Morris, congregational minister at First United Church from 1982 to 1989.

Barry Morris was born in Vancouver and grew up in the Kerrisdale area where he was a member of Kerrisdale Presbyterian Church. He received a BA from UBC in 1964 and then, having won a Rockefeller scholarship, he studied theology at the Chicago Theological Seminary. Following his first year of theological studies, Barry worked at the Christian Resource Centre (CRC), an outreach ministry in the Regent Park housing project in Toronto. This experience encouraged him to proceed with his studies, and he returned to Chicago for another year. He then seized an opportunity to work for fifteen months in San Jose, California, in a special outreach ministry to homeless and alienated youth. He completed his final year of theological studies in Chicago in 1968 and returned to Toronto, where he was ordained as a United Church minister and became part of the team at the CRC. After six years there, Barry moved to Winnipeg where he spent seven years in a new outreach ministry established as St. Matthews–Maryland Community Ministry.

the mission and participated in the programs and projects that were directed by other team members. In *First Things First,* Bob Stewart described Barry as "an astonishing bundle of free-floating compassion . . . who always knew when to break the rules when they were inappropriate."[43]

In the summer of 1983 Elsie Rosenberg, who had been on staff from 1968 to 1976, re-joined the staff as a part-time pastoral visitor. Geniene Elliot joined the staff as receptionist in January 1983 and became office coordinator in June. She continued in this role until July 1984 when she moved to Hazelton. In 1986, looking back on the part played by the office staff in the ministries of First United, John Cashore wrote that:

> A significant part . . . has been the ministry of the office staff to the community. Not only do they do an outstanding job of looking after our community and program staff as well as the ministers, they also serve the hundreds of people who come to us for help.[44]

For two hundred of those who came to the front office window each week, First United was the only mailing address they had because many of the rooming houses and hotels where they lived did not provide security for tenant mail. As a result, the staff at First United was regularly overwhelmed on government cheque days, but they always remained concerned for the needs of each individual.

During the early 1980s, the United Church began a program of assigning theological students as interns to selected churches across Canada. These appointments could be for the four summer months or the eight months from September to April. Over the next twenty-five years, many students had the privilege of being interns at First United. In 1983, when reviewing his first few years at First United Church, John Cashore wrote the following about the intern program for *First Things First*:

> The placement of theological students in year-long or summer assignments at First Church has been one of the significant developments of recent years . . . The work they accomplished and the things they learned were much more profound than anything we planned. One of our students, Bill Bruce, was preaching his second sermon in 1982 at the morning service. Just as he was arriving at the climax of his sermon, a man approached the chancel steps. Bill looked up, somewhat startled.
>
> The man said in a loud voice, "Pray for Bobby!"
>
> "We'll pray for your friend in a few minutes, sir," said Bill.
>
> Bill looked up again and the man had moved so close that the two of them were standing nose to nose.
>
> "Pray for Bobby now!" he demanded.
>
> Bill's next words were profound and simple: "Let us pray . . ."
>
> We all learned something that day.[45]

On May 5, 1983, a provincial election returned the Social Credit government of Bill Bennett for another term, and two months later this government introduced their "Restraint Budget," accompanied by twenty-six prospective bills. The crucial legislation fell into three categories: bills that undermined trade-union practices and the status of collective bargaining, especially in the public sector; those that abolished watchdog-type bodies (for example, the Rentalsman's office); and those that cut social services. Thus, it threatened labour and a host of underprivileged groups, including welfare recipients, women and children, the handicapped and ethnic minorities. In response, the BC Federation of Labour, allied with community and advocacy groups, organized a massive protest movement known as "Solidarity." It was composed of Operation Solidarity, which was the trade-union wing, and the Solidarity Coalition, made up of churches and social agencies and welfare rights organizations.

For three months Solidarity protested the proposed legislation with huge marches and rallies that brought tens of thousands of people into the streets of Vancouver and onto the lawns of the provincial legislature. A weekly newspaper was launched to voice the peoples' opposition, the Vancouver offices of the provincial cabinet were occupied, and at the end of August fifty thousand people attended a protest rally at Empire Stadium. But in the provincial capital, Victoria, all-night sittings had been used to "legislate by exhaustion," and debate had been stifled by

---

Persons receiving handicapped pensions had been permitted to receive $50 per month as a supplement to their pension if they worked a total of twenty hours a month for a non-profit organization. This allowance, known as the Community Involvement Program, was one of the many cancelled by the new legislation. A "Fight Back Committee" sent letters and petitions to government asking that the program be restored since it was important for the participants and also for the agencies where they worked. However, the minister responsible for Human Resources indicated that she expected the churches and community groups to "pick up the slack."[46]

closure so that by late October many of the restraint bills had been passed into law.

Knowing that many government workers were scheduled to be fired when the BC Government Employees Union (BCGEU) contract expired on October 31, the union took legal strike action on November 1. At the same time Solidarity began organizing an escalating series of public sector strikes, which threatened to put two hundred thousand workers on the streets. Then on November 7 all the teachers in the province were called out on strike and it appeared that a general strike would follow. But over the weekend of November 11 to 13, the leadership of Operation Solidarity negotiated an end to the job action, abandoning the movement's broad aim of forcing the repeal of the entire legislative package for the narrower end of gaining a contract for the BCGEU. Once again the poor and the handicapped were the losers.

Along with other churches and agencies that worked in the Downtown Eastside community, First United still hoped the government would reconsider the punitive legislation introduced in July. But that did not happen, and month by month an increasing number of families and single men and women were evicted from their rooms or confronted by huge increases in rent. As a result, First United Church became one of the founding member organizations in the sixteen-member End Legislated Poverty (ELP) Coalition, which was developed to address the totally inadequate level of support for those on social assistance. Linda Ervin and Leslie Black, both from the First United staff, were deeply involved from the beginning. From late 1984 to early 1986 they took part in education events and press conferences and made appearances before municipal councils and provincial politicians from both government and opposition parties. The ELP coalition also worked with the BC Teacher's Federation to develop a high school social studies resource unit called "Poverty in BC." They knew that it would take strong social advocacy to pressure politicians into creating systems where the poor, the unemployed, the elderly and the handicapped would be treated with respect and compassion.

Unfortunately, ELP's earnest message was not getting through to those who could make changes, and social assistance rates remained intolerably low. When it became obvious that it would take much more to gain the attention of the public, a plan was developed to recruit someone prominent to live on the social assistance rate of $350 for one month in the Downtown Eastside. In January 1986 Emery Barnes, MLA for Vancouver Centre and a former football player and then social worker, heard about this plan and volunteered to take it on. At last the media's attention was caught, and the coalition asked Leslie Black to be the media liaison person, possibly because First United was seen to be closer to politically neutral than some of the other coalition members. The publicity achieved through Barnes's month on social assistance helped to communicate the coalition's basic message that current social assistance rates were inadequate, even inhumane, to a huge segment of the general population. This project of mass education at last shattered the myth that living on welfare was easy.

In 1986 John Cashore made the decision to enter the world of partisan politics and was chosen as the NDP candidate in the provincial riding of Maillardville–Coquitlam. Because an election was anticipated for the spring of 1987, the Oversight Committee at First United made arrangements for John to have a leave of absence from January to June 1987. However, this plan had to be hurriedly set aside when an election was called instead in October 1986. Because John was the successful candidate, his resignation from First United took effect on October 31, 1986. At the end of November the First United community held a farewell party for John and Sharon Cashore, though, as with most of the men and women who have worked at First United Church, it is never really farewell.

The nine months that followed John Cashore's departure from First United were especially challenging for the staff and the volunteer members of the Oversight Committee, who found themselves, in the absence of a superintendent, doing a good deal of a superintendent's work. Eunice Williams, a long-time member of West Point Grey United Church and veteran member of many presbytery and conference committees, had been chairperson of the Oversight Committee since it was established in 1976. Now she felt obliged to be available on an almost daily basis to provide leadership and make necessary decisions. Much of the administrative responsibility during this period was carried by the financial services officer, George Maaren, who had joined the staff in January 1985. Then in the summer of 1987 the situation became even more difficult when, for entirely separate reasons, Linda Ervin, Beth Jennings and Leslie Black all left First Church and moved on to other challenges. Linda returned to university to complete a degree and then became a member of a new team ministry at Trinity United Church in Kitsilano; Beth accepted the offer of a position with a community agency; and Leslie and her partner, Henri Lock, left to be part of a team ministry in the very special First Nations village of Kispiox, BC.

= CHAPTER 7 =

1987–1997

Jim Elliot, Superintendent, 1987–1997

The Reverend Jim Elliot began his ten-year ministry as superintendent of First United Church on August 1, 1987. He describes his leadership during those years as pastoral, program-oriented and heavily committed to working as part of a team. It was a time when even more volunteers were recruited and made to feel welcome and important in the First United community.

An incident that occurred just after Jim's arrival at First United gives a strong hint of the tone that would be set there during the next decade. He had been asked to sign a banning order for a man who had kicked a door in and said abusive things to one of the volunteers. No one knew his name, so he was just referred to as "Boots." But Jim was not happy about banning people he did not know, and he decided to talk with the man. Jim soon realized that Boots was suffering from some kind of brain damage, probably the result of alcohol abuse, and instead of banning him, Jim asked him if he would help the church by being on the lookout for abusive behaviour and reporting it if necessary. Boots happily accepted this assignment. His own behaviour turned from negative to positive, and he was still a cooperative member of the community ten years later. Shortly after Jim's encounter with Boots, the police had to be called in to deal with another person who couldn't be controlled. This prompted Jim to write this poem:

> There is such a feeling of failure
> when we have to call the police
> and have someone removed from the church.
> Often they are obnoxious, abusive, right out of it.
> Yet through the fog, the booze, the drugs, the illness
> they have arrived at the church.
>
> What is it that drives them here?
>
> Are we safe, caring, a soft touch, or just here?
> Whatever it is, they just come and sometimes
> we just can't handle the behaviour.
> Are we failures? Or just part of reality?
>
> It doesn't really matter. It just hurts.

THE WISH CENTRE: A MAJOR NEW INITIATIVE

Within a few months of Jim Elliot's arrival, he, his staff and the First United Oversight Board, as the committee was now called, were faced with an unexpected challenge. A request for help came from the Anglican Street Ministry for Youth, which had opened a drop-in centre in 1984 at St. Michael's Anglican Church in the Mount Pleasant community. During its first year of operation it had been open to both young men and women as a place of safety from the violence on the streets, but it was soon discovered that some of the men who dropped in to the centre

Jim Elliot was born in Edson, Alberta, in 1933. His Scottish father was a coal miner, and Jim was raised in a series of Alberta coal-mining communities, attending eleven schools in twelve years. But his father was determined that no son of his would enter the mines, so after high school, as the first step in an accounting career, Jim worked for three years for the Canadian Utilities company in Drumheller. During these years he played baseball, sang in a church choir and was active in the church young people's association, and he also began to privately contemplate studying to be a minister. In the end it was the church janitor, who also happened to be an elder in the church, who played a significant role in encouraging him to take the final step in that direction.

Jim began his studies at the University of Alberta and later entered St. Stephen's College, spending summers in student mission posts and taking leadership positions in church youth camps. He was ordained in 1960 and began his ministry serving congregations in rural Alberta. In 1963 he moved to Sherwood Park United Church in Edmonton and later to St. David's United Church in Calgary. When he came to BC, he was the minister at South Arm United Church in Richmond and then at Highlands United in North Vancouver. From 1984 to 1987 Jim served as the minister at Hazelton, Kispiox and Kitsegukla in northern BC.

were the very people who had treated the women violently on the streets. It was then restricted to women drop-ins and women volunteers only. After the centre had been in operation for two years, the parish council prepared to close it as they wanted the space for other programs. They were, however, persuaded to allow it to remain open, but since the contract of the outreach worker responsible for the centre, David Dranchuk, would finish in mid-1987, they were unsure

The Reverend Jim Elliot, superintendent of First United Church from 1987 to 1997.

about having it carry on beyond that date with only volunteers in charge.

By this time the Mount Pleasant Neighbourhood Association, allied with a number of other community organizations, had formulated an "anti-hooker battle plan" that emphasized putting pressure on city council and the Vancouver Police Department to rid the district of prostitutes entirely. The police department responded by instituting annual summer-time task forces to discourage the sex trade in that area. As a result of this action combined with the neighbourhood association's determined harassment of city council, St. Michael's parish council asked the Anglican Street Ministry for Youth to seek a new venue for the drop-in centre. In turning to First United for help, the Street Ministry was no doubt aware of Jim Hatherly's street ministry project back in 1981 and the work of Barry Morris and some members of the First Church congregation who had attempted to relate in a supportive way to women involved in the sex trade downtown. It was, therefore, logical for them to ask First United Church to provide space for a drop-in centre for women of the streets.

Jim Elliot and his team were sympathetic to the need, but the Oversight Board had first to be sure the church's liability insurance would be adequate and that it would be possible to isolate the southwest corner of the church so that the drop-in centre could maintain privacy. After careful consultation and discussion, they agreed to make space available. This decision was appreciated by all those associated with the program. In its new location, the Women's Information and Safe House (WISH) Drop-in Centre became an independent organization that used space made available by the church. The WISH website acknowledges the centre's connection with First United:

It was only through the generosity of First United Church in donating space that WISH was able to survive. First United welcomed

WISH on December 4, 1987, at Hastings and Gore in the heart of the Downtown Eastside.

The mission statement of the WISH program reads: "To increase the health, safety and well-being of women working in the sex trade in Vancouver's Downtown Eastside." To that end, the program instituted in 1987 ran from four to eleven p.m. each day and offered coffee, washrooms, showers and hot meals, as well as advice about "bad dates," friendship and support from sensitive volunteers. Among those volunteers was Ina Roelants, who had moved to Vancouver from Montreal shortly after the drop-in centre was established at St. Michael's and volunteered five days a week for the next eight years. She is credited with keeping WISH going through its difficult early years; in fact, according to David Dranchuk, it would not have survived without her.[47]

Many stories are told about the way in which the women of the WISH centre subsequently identified First United as "their" church. On one occasion, a WISH centre regular heard that there had been a break-in at the church the previous night and that a fax machine had been stolen. She said she knew who had done this and was prepared to finger the man "who had the nerve to steal things from our church." On another occasion, early in the evening, one of the regular WISH community members noticed a stranger trying to break into the car of one of the First United staff members. She chased the intruder away from the parking lot and rushed back up to the church office to alert the community worker.

The partnership between First United and the centre lasted for more than twenty years, ending in November 2008 when the WISH Drop-in Centre Society moved into its own facility two blocks away. In 2003 WISH had been chosen by VanCity Credit Union as the charity to receive a donation of $1 million, and after several years of searching and planning, the society made arrangements with the City of Vancouver to rent thirty-five hundred square feet of space on the second floor of the warehouse where the Vancouver Police Department stores evidence. The new address is 330 Alexander Street; the ten-year lease costs the society one dollar per year. The million-dollar gift from VanCity was used for renovations, furnishings and equipment.

When Jim Elliot arrived at First United in August 1987, Norine Mawer and George Maaren, who had begun their work there just a few weeks apart in early 1985, were providing continuity and stability for the mission's social services. Earlier in her life Norine Mawer had worked in the public relations field, and when her children were small, she had been heavily involved as a volunteer in the work of Highlands United Church in North Vancouver. When she first began working at First United Church in 1985, she shared the receptionist position with Leslie Campbell, but within a year she was appointed office coordinator; by then she knew most of the people of the community and had a good grasp of the working habits of all the staff. George Maaren came to

Norine Mawer, office staff for 21 years, retired in 2006.

First United as the financial services officer, and he worked hard to keep on top of the finances, though he also gave great support to the administration of the Dugout. For two decades, Norine Mawer, in the office, and George Maaren, in financial services, played remarkable roles in guiding the church through the constantly changing Downtown Eastside world. (George Maaren retired in 2001; Norine Mawer served

as First United's assistant exec-
utive-director from 2001 until
her own retirement in 2006.)

At the beginning of 1988,
Geniene Elliot, who had been
on the church staff as office
coordinator a few years earlier,
was appointed program coordinator, and for the next several years she provided lively
leadership to a wide range of
activities. Many other men and
women through the years kept
the building clean and safe and
the office running smoothly.
During the 1960s and 1970s

George Maaren served as the financial
services officer at First United from
1985 to 2002.

there had been two maintenance staff members, one of them living in the church apartment, but as the building aged and the
activities increased, additional staff were required on a part-time
basis. In the early years of the new building the office was staffed
by a receptionist, bookkeeper and office coordinator, in addition
to secretarial support, in those pre-computer days. The ministries of several long-serving office staff members were very important to the mission: Pat Clarke, Erma Francis, Joan Birchall,
Ann Farrell, Eleanor Jackson, Margaret Maxwell, Jack Cameron,
Audrey Stowell, Dorothy Manson, Geniene Elliot, Jean Wooley,
Helen Ross and Donna Currie.

FUNDRAISING

Each year First United Church was forced to increase its fundraising efforts to keep up with inflation and to sponsor new initiatives. In 1987 a novel fundraising project was conceived by
David Jiles and his partner, Carol Denny, friends of John Cashore.

While eating breakfast one Saturday morning at a restaurant on Granville Island, David decided that he could prepare just as good a breakfast at home, then invite friends to share it and at the same time bring a donation for First United Church. So they invited a host of friends to a "Porridge Breakfast" one Saturday morning a few weeks before Christmas and served them porridge, coffee, muffins and fruit. There was great sociability at this event, and without any speeches or fanfare to exhort guests to give, people quietly drifted past the bowl on the mantle and deposited their donations. Some members of the First United Church staff also attended, answering questions and engaging the guests in conversation about the church's current projects. This tradition continued uninterrupted for the next twenty years, generating both financial support and new friends for the work of First United Church.

PROGRAMS

Although the early months of Jim Elliot's administration were marked by the arrival of new staff and the introduction of some major new programs, existing activities were also maintained. The Handicapped Program had been ably coordinated for many years by Beth Jennings, and after her departure from staff in 1987, volunteers who had been part of the program for many years stepped in to lead. Fortunately, one of these volunteers was Bill Hennessy, who helped initiate the program a decade earlier; he had moved to the Okanagan in 1980 for health reasons but was now back living in the Lower Mainland. Twice each week, forty or fifty people gathered at the church for activities designed to meet their needs for recreation and fellowship. These gatherings also provided opportunities for the church advocates to become better acquainted with the men and women who often needed encouragement and support.

The most dramatic change to any existing program came at

the very end of the 1980s. A grant from the Canadian Mental Health Association in the spring of 1989 had funded a survey of unmet needs in the First United Church community, but there was a very short time-frame between the awarding of the grant and the required completion date for the study. Fortunately, Pat Dyer, a trusted volunteer at First United and a mature student at UBC, was not only well qualified but also available to carry out the survey. Many of the people she interviewed participated in First United's Handicapped Program, but they felt it was not meeting their needs because they had mental health challenges but not necessarily physical handicaps. They wanted a program where they would find a sense of family and friendship, and that would provide a meeting place and time of their own. So it was that the Family Friendship Place was born, named by the participants themselves. To accommodate the new program, the Happy Hours weekly social fellowship was discontinued; for several years attendance had been seriously declining, because many seniors were anxious about coming to

Joseph Thibault, Cari Copeman-Haynes, and Bill Hennesy in the mid-1990s.

In the early 1990s BC Conference archivist Bob Stewart was asked to speak at the fall gathering of the United Church Men's Groups called AOTS. He talked about the importance of the archives and then shared some of his thoughts about the Family Friendship Place program at First United Church where Bob both lived and worked at that time.

The Family Friendship Place program at First United Church brings together a group of people whose lives are filled with emotional and psychological difficulties. It is a pretty tough group to work with and several staff members and volunteers are involved each week. The program does seem to provide precisely a family and friendship setting for people who have often had neither family nor friendship.

But an interesting aspect of the group that I really like is that they make the decisions. They have a fair bit to say about what they are going to do. As individuals, most of them have never really had many opportunities to decide things for themselves, and here they are able to. It is not easy, and I am sure that things might run a lot smoother if we simply laid on a program, but a part of the idea of this program is for people to begin to experiment with taking charge of parts of their own lives. And it seems to work. I am not at all sure that many of the individual members of the group are going to have lives that have a very happy ending, but I do believe that the Family Friendship Place program is helping them to become a little less dependent, a little more independent and interdependent as they go through life. And in the process, I am sure that First United Church is also learning something from those we serve. We learn that if we are interested in longer term solutions, we have to take the time to nurture that independence and interdependence, rather than look for the quick fix. What I see in Family Friendship Place that attracts me is that it seems to be a good experiment in people discovering that they have some power to do some things for themselves. They are becoming empowered. On occasion they invite one of the community workers to join them and talk about issues that affect how they live. So they discuss legislation relating to the rights of the handicapped or they discuss welfare rates. Last summer they wrote to the premier of the province. Sometimes they simply decide where they are going to go for a picnic. It may not seem like much to us, but for many of these people, their lives have been a pattern of always being told what and when they were going to eat, where they were going to go, and what they would do.[48]

the church on their own, when the streets held more and more homeless people who also occupied space in the church during the day.

Many of the participants in the new Family Friendship Place were people who found it difficult to take part in social or recreation activities in regular community programs. Therefore, although First United Church staff and volunteers would provide the basic structure for this new program, the members themselves planned the activities to meet their own needs. Joseph Thibault, one of the long-time volunteers in the program, recently displayed his many pictures of Family Friendship Place activities. He has witnessed that week after week, for many years, this was the high point in the lives of the dozens of men and women from the church community who participated.

The friendly, open-door atmosphere of programs like Family Friendship Place sometimes led to unexpected problems. One day George Maaren, First United's financial officer, heard a community member describing a strange scene she had just witnessed a few blocks from the church. A man, very drunk, was being pushed up and down the street in a wheelchair by a woman who was having a hilarious time with this adventure. Taking a quick look around, George realized that the church wheelchair was missing from its usual place. He ran down the few blocks to Cordova Street and found what he was looking for. He allegedly announced, "This is *my* chair!" He

Joyce Brown served for fifteen years as the coordinator of volunteers at First United Church.

then proceeded to push the chair's occupant to the detox centre before pushing the empty chair back to the church.

A Native Cultural Development Team was created in 1988, spearheaded by Jacqueline Smith, Tracey Laroque and Steve Johnson; every Thursday evening up to one hundred and fifty people came to First United for native drumming, dancing and singing, followed by coffee and sometimes food. Then on September 22, 1989, the team hosted a Native Friendship Day that was attended by five hundred and forty people and included a salmon feast followed by a pow-wow.

Geniene Elliot worked with Ariel Creighton to organize and lead a parenting group, which helped Downtown Eastside mothers deal with the many challenges they faced raising children in this difficult urban setting. When one of the mothers, a woman struggling with mental health problems, had to be hospitalized, Geniene, Ariel and other staff members looked after her young child for the next few months. A few months later, that same mother, now in much better health, became a member of the committee choosing a new minister for the congregation at First United. In the committee's interview with a prospective minister, she asked what for her was a very important question: "If I have to go into hospital again, will you help to look after my child?"

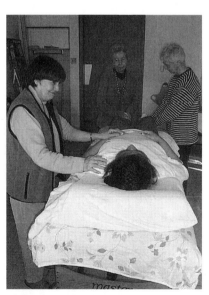

Mary Al Lay, Carole Kidd and Sandra Pond reach many community members with the ministry of Healing Touch.

During this period Geniene Elliot and Ariel Creighton also introduced "Healing Touch" to First United Church community members, and they encouraged other qualified people to come as volunteers to provide healing touch on a regular basis. In the mid-1990s, Lee McKim and Mary Al Lay began to offer it on a weekly basis in a quiet room near the Gore Avenue entrance to the church; in 2010 this ministry was still being provided by Mary Al Lay, Marg King and Carole Kidd every Thursday.

Another successful program, spearheaded by Doree Piercy and carried out largely by volunteers, was called "Give-a-Gift." By the late 1980s the church had deliberately moved away from giving out large, expensive Christmas hampers because well-meaning donors too often included items that were inappropriate for needy families. The new program provided small gift bags for all of the community members who regularly participated in one or more of the First United programs. Churches throughout the Lower Mainland contributed both selected items and funds to purchase the gifts, volunteers packaged them during Advent, and the gifts were then distributed during the traditional Christmas program. Up to five hundred people were thus acknowledged each year.

Volunteers also supplied leadership for another Christmas program that developed over a period of years. In the weeks before Christmas, the church provided cards and postage so that community members could send greetings to friends or family members. When required, volunteers assisted to prepare the message. For some of the senders, this was the first time in many years that they had made any attempt to communicate with family members, but the responses to some of their messages were heartwarming.

Doree Piercy has been a volunteer coordinator of the Christmas Give-a-Gift project since 1987.

The success of this service provided one more reason to make the administration of the church's mail more efficient. With the introduction of quarterly GST cheques for low income people, the number of people already receiving their mail in care of First United had swelled to over four hundred. A new system had to be put in place: now when the cheques arrived, the reception window was closed for two hours while the mail was sorted and then three staff members shared in handing out mail to the members of the community who had waited patiently in line. But in addition to those people coming to collect mail, another two hundred and fifty or more approached the window each day with other requests for help.

Another program that had started in the early 1980s but was enlarged during Jim Elliot's time at First United was assistance with filling out income tax forms. Knowledgeable and faithful volunteers came to the church during February, March and April to help community members complete their tax returns. As the years went by, more and more people came for tax help until several hundred tax returns were being submitted through the church annually.

The serving of nourishing soup at 8:30 a.m. had been a feature at First United for a decade when Jim Elliot began his ministry in 1987. Up to two hundred people enjoyed the soup and bread, and many of them returned later in the morning for coffee and sandwiches. But in the late 1980s Jim's team decided that right after the serving of soup, there should be an opportunity for people to gather in the church sanctuary for a Bible reading or singing a hymn. Only a few people regularly took advantage of this, but it became a significant event for those who attended. From Monday to Friday, at 8:45 a.m., in full view of the community members lining up at the front office window, a handful of staff and community members gathered around a table to read, pray and sing. For many of them this was their church.

Nourishing soup is served at 8:30 a.m. every day of the week.

SECURITY STAFF

Occasional violent incidents in the lineups at First United were not uncommon. Fights sometimes broke out among those wait-

ing for the phone near the front desk window. It is a free phone available to all for local calls, although there is a clearly marked time limit on them. Fights also broke out in the morning soup lineup. Each time it happened, staff members were called to help, always hoping to avoid further upset and violence. On one occasion a minister helped to break up a fight on the Gore Avenue steps. Less than an hour later,

Kevin Abrahams was the first security officer employed at First United Church, shown here in the mid-1990s.

after the minister had returned to his office, the attacker came back, stabbed his victim and left him to die in the alley behind the church.

Unfortunately, by the mid-1990s fights had become more frequent and more severe. Standing in ever-lengthening queues made for shorter and shorter tempers. Perhaps more important was the addition of crack cocaine to the standard drug mix of alcohol and heroin available in the Downtown Eastside, which produced an unprecedented level of sudden and unpredictable outbursts of violence. The regular staff could no longer cope. An altogether new staff position had to be created and filled by a person with a new set of attributes. Kevin Abrahams was hired as the church's first security staff member, and he used his physical presence and his unflappable demeanor to minimize the disputes that inevitably sprang up in the corridors and lineups. The male clergy and community workers who had been called on to handle noisy disputes in the past were especially grateful when Kevin arrived.

ADVOCACY

Since First United's earliest outreach efforts in the 1920s, helping community members navigate the confusing waters of government bureaucracy has been part of the church's social service agenda. Under Bill Hennessy's leadership in the 1970s, First United began to call this service "advocacy," and it has remained at the centre of the church's ministry. At any given time at least two staff members concentrate on advocacy work. In the early 1980s Alan Alvare, Linda Ervin and Leslie Black each carried heavy advocacy workloads, and when Linda and Leslie left, Karen Howe joined Alan in this section of the work. When Alan left in 1990, others came on staff for short terms, and in 1991 Leslie Campbell and Stephen Gray joined the team and became the anchors for several years. For three years Evelyn Rigby was also an advocate, leaving this position to be the minister at Skidegate on Queen Charlotte Islands (Haida Gwaii). She was followed for one year by Barbara Douglas. Each of them brought their individual gifts and skills to the task. Collectively, they took very seriously the obstacles facing many of the community's members, and with patience and wisdom helped them to achieve a measure of justice. As paralegal advo-

Stephen Gray, an advocate at First United Church from 1991 to present.

cates, they frequently faced residential tenancy issues, serious health-related challenges, and often a combination of problems in which the seemingly impenetrable maze of bureaucratic requirements overwhelmed and immobilized fragile, marginalized men and women.

THE CONGREGATION

The late 1980s and early 1990s was a critical time for the small worshipping congregation at First United Church. Since it was difficult to sustain a Sunday school in the Downtown Eastside, families with children seldom chose to worship there, and as a result, the Sunday morning congregation was small. However, both clergy staff members still took part in the morning worship, although the primary responsibility lay with Barry Morris. The broadcast services had been discontinued in the early 1980s. The contract for the sale of the radio licence to station CKWX in 1938 had stipulated, among other things, that the station would provide up to six hours per week of broadcast time to the United Church, but over the years the amount of time the church used had shrunk to three hours per week and then to one hour. From 1981 to 1983 the station and the church met many times to talk about the gradual drop in the size of the listening audience as well as shifts in the station's programming focus. They finally agreed to discontinue the broadcast of church services altogether. The team at First United hoped this would not cause a serious decline in donations for its mission work.

When Barry Morris left First United in 1989, the Reverend Gary Paterson was called to provide leadership to the congregation and share in other aspects of the mission, but with a heavy emphasis on the former. This proved to be a time of growth for the congregation, no doubt related to Gary's dynamic preaching and worship leadership. David Hodge, who chaired the congregational board for many years, speaks of "Gary's remarkable ability to preach with dramatic energy and also to listen carefully to any members of the community who wanted to share their stories with him."[49] Some staff families with children now became active in the congregation, and for a time there was a revival of the Sunday school and a clear sense that the congregation was still

Gary Paterson was born in November 1949 in Whitehorse, Yukon. His father was in the Canadian army and the family moved many times. He attended schools in Victoria, Germany and Toronto and finished his final year of high school at Winston Churchill School in Vancouver, where he received a Governor General's Silver Medal for British Columbia in 1966. He graduated with an honours BA in English at UBC, completed a master's degree in English at Queen's University and taught English at UBC for two years. In 1973 he was awarded a Rockefeller scholarship, studied theology at Boston University for two years and followed this with a year on the program staff of the Naramata Centre. He completed his preparation for the ordained ministry at the Vancouver School of Theology in 1977. His first ministry was the Winfield, Oyama and Lumby pastoral charge in the north Okanagan; he then moved to Marpole United in Vancouver. Just prior to coming to First United he was a member of the BC Conference staff team responsible for youth and young adult programs.

an important part of the First United Church ministry. In addition to his work with the congregation, Gary was also a sensitive and caring chaplain to the staff members and key volunteers.

When Gary Paterson left in 1993 to become minister of Ryerson United Church in Vancouver, he was replaced by the Very Reverend Robert Smith, former moderator of the United Church of Canada, who had been the minister at Shaughnessy Heights United Church in Vancouver since 1982. His responsibilities at First United were divided equally between the congregation and the outreach programs of the church, but to both of them he brought his strong pastoral gifts and his passion for social justice. In addition to his work with the congregation, Bob was chaplain to the staff and, during the time when Jim Elliot was off work due to illness, he shared with George Maaren the superintendent's responsibilities. When interviewed by the *United Church Observer* a few years after his retirement, Bob said that his years at First United were "the richest experience of my life . . . It is the place with the most authentic expression of faith in action that I have encountered."[50]

Since the 1920s First United Church has been known as "the Church of the Open Door," but the term "open door" took on a new meaning in 1993 when the church invoked the medieval concept of sanctuary. Fatima Bibi Khan, a 66-year-old woman from Fiji, was faced with a deportation order issued by Immigration Canada. She had come to Canada in 1985 on a visitor's permit and soon

The Reverend Bob Smith, who served at First United from 1993 to 1998.

Bob Smith was born in Montreal in May 1934. Both his father, Douglas, and his grandfather, Robert, were United Church ministers. Bob began his education in Brockville, but the family moved to Hamilton when he was ten years old and to Edmonton in 1952 when Bob was eighteen. He completed his BA at the University of Alberta and his BD degree at St. Stephen's College, Edmonton. In 1957–58 he was the president of the University of Alberta Student Union. When he graduated from St. Stephen's College in 1958, he married Ellen Maguire, was ordained as a minister of the United Church of Canada and settled as resident minister in Fort St. John, BC. Three years later he moved to Trinity United Church in Edmonton, after which he went to Boston for three years and received his ThD degree from Boston University.

In 1968 Bob returned to Canada as minister of Richmond Hill United Church, moved to Eglinton United Church in Toronto in 1974 and Shaughnessy Heights United Church in Vancouver in 1982. Early in his Vancouver ministry he was elected moderator of the United Church of Canada and from August 1984 to August 1986 provided inspiring leadership to the church throughout Canada. It was his privilege to make the apology on behalf of the United Church of Canada to Canada's First Nations People at the 1986 meeting of the General Council.

afterward was diagnosed with breast cancer. Her application for permanent residence was turned down on medical grounds, and her son's application to sponsor her was mysteriously lost. Despite a letter from her doctor indicating that her cancer was in remission, her application was still rejected. She was granted sanctuary by the congregation of First United on May 25, 1993. Family members came to the church to cook for her almost every day, but she was unable to leave the church building and was desperately lonely and frustrated.

Unfortunately, the year 1993 ended with a frightening experience for some of the First United staff and for Fatima. As it was New Year's Eve, the church office and doors had been closed just after lunch, although George Maaren, the financial officer, Norine Mawer, the office coordinator and Leslie Campbell, an advocate, were still working in the office. At 3:30 Bob Stewart arrived back at the church office from his work at the church archives, and as the four of them chatted, Norine suddenly noticed black smoke pouring out of the partially underground parking garage. A closer look established that this was a serious fire, and she rushed back to the office, told the others to phone 911 and then ran to the south end of the church to rescue Fatima, who was all alone in her room that day. Although Fatima was at risk of being arrested if she left the building, Norine concluded that she had to get her out of the church for her safety. Two doors east of the church was a hairdressing salon, and soon a frightened Fatima was settled there in a chair, safe for the moment. It happened that Leslie Campbell's vehicle was the only car in the parking area, and although the fire department arrived in time to prevent the fire from spreading from the garage to the church, her car was totally destroyed. It had been torched.

Sadly, after one year in sanctuary, Fatima Bibi Khan died,

The Very Reverend Bob Smith wrote the following story about his time at First United for *First Things First*:

It was one of those days when I was responsible for "hospitality," spending my morning, armed only with a two-way radio and my radiant and sincere smile, roaming the halls to welcome people and to be a curb, if necessary, on their—shall we say?—more boisterous activities, when I was stopped by a small man who, as he accosted me, looked around (I thought) somewhat furtively.

"You work here?" he said.

Stifling a smart response, I acknowledged that I did. "What can I do for you?" I said. "Well, it's this way," he said. "I was here one day last month and youse guys kind of helped me out."

I surreptitiously fingered the loonies in my pocket and calculated how many I was likely to part with.

He continued, "Yeah, I had just come to town and I had this great big backpack, which was really draggin' me down. Youse guys let me leave my backpack in the office for two whole days, and—you know what, mister? In those two days I was able to find me a room, and now I've got a job. So I just wanted to come around and say, like, thanks a lot, eh? It was a big help."

"Thanks for saying thanks," said I and went on my way, glad that it was my turn, that morning, to be on the receiving end of such a gift.[51]

having been allowed to spend only the final few days of her life in her son's home.

In 1997 health concerns forced Jim Elliot to resign from his work at First United Church one year before his anticipated retirement date. In the June 1997 issue of *First Things First*, Bob Smith described "The Elliot Years," with the following highlights:

> Jim was a passionate proponent of justice, a spokesperson for the ones who had no voice . . . [His] style of leadership was collegial, walking beside rather than walking ahead . . . [He] was quick-witted and there was a lot of laughing when he was near . . . Jim was an able preacher, a gifted story-teller.[52]

Jim Elliot was a blessing to the First United Church community and, in turn, he was blessed by the people of the Downtown Eastside. Like so many others before him and since, he described the experience of working at First United Church as "life-changing."

⇒ CHAPTER 8 ⇐

1997–2007

The Ruth Wright Years, 1997–2007

Ruth Wright assumed the leadership role at First United Church on August 1, 1997. She had been a summer intern at First United Church three years earlier and was therefore moving into a community that was familiar. In a letter written in early June 2010 in which she reflects on her arrival at First United, Ruth wrote:

> My predecessor, Jim Elliot, had gathered around him an amazing staff ready to take on any challenge that faced them. They were dedicated, overworked and, in some cases, unable to admit to themselves or others that they were trying to do too much . . . Times were changing in the community at a great rate. Persons with alcohol addictions were declining proportionately, and those with addictions to other drugs—hard drugs—were skyrocketing. AIDS was rampant in the community, and multi-agency action was required, for which we provided space, energy and shared leadership.[53]

The Reverend Dr. Ruth Wright, lead minister at First United Church from 1997 to 2007. BAYNE STANLEY PHOTO

During the early years of Ruth Wright's ministry at First United, recognition was growing that the number of women missing from the Downtown Eastside was increasing. In 1999 a woman named Maggie deVries approached Ruth to request that a memorial service be held at the church for her sister, Sarah, who had been missing since April 13, 1998. Preparations for this service soon led to the involvement of several other grieving families, and on May 12, 1999, some four hundred people packed First United Church. "This service," wrote Ruth Wright, "was a precipitating factor in the establishment of a special integrated police task force to investigate the disappearances, and it generated energy toward cooperative approaches among the agencies working with women."[54] As a result of the memorial service, Ruth developed a special relationship with several of the grieving families. She was later asked by the

Ruth Wright was born in Moncton, New Brunswick, in 1947 and was educated in Stoney Creek and Moncton. She took her first two degrees (BSc and BEd) at the University of New Brunswick before attending the University of Ottawa for an MA and a PhD. She taught at the University of Saskatchewan, St. Francis Xavier and the University of Ottawa where she became chair of the department of Educational Administration in 1987 and served a two-year term as president of the Canadian Society for the Study of Education. In 1991 she made the decision to become an ordained minister and began theological studies at Queen's University. She gained experience as a student weekend-supply minister in the small community of Apple Hill, while she took basic courses at Queen's and taught part-time in her old faculty in Ottawa. In 1995 she was ordained and became the minister of the Summerford–Moreton's Harbour pastoral charge in Newfoundland.

provincial government's Victim Services department to lead a healing service for the families of the missing women who were awaiting a verdict from the initial Robert Pickton trial.

At the same time that Ruth Wright, her team and First United's Oversight Board were involved in urging the police to investigate the missing women of the Downtown Eastside, they were also deeply concerned about the rapid spread of HIV-AIDs in

---

THE "FOUR PILLARS DRUG STRATEGY" OF THE CITY OF VANCOUVER

Prevention
Promoting healthy families and communities, protecting child and youth development, preventing or delaying the start of substance use among young people and reducing harm associated with substance use. Successful prevention efforts aim to improve the health of the general population and reduce differences in health between groups of people.

Treatment
Offering individuals access to services that help them to come to terms with problem substance use and lead healthier lives, including outpatient and peer-based counseling, methadone programs, daytime and residential treatment, housing support and ongoing medical care.

Harm reduction
Reducing the spread of deadly communicable diseases, preventing drug overdose deaths, increasing substance users' contact with health care services and drug treatment programs and reducing consumption of drugs in the street.

Enforcement
Recognizing the need for peace and quiet, public order and safety in the Downtown Eastside and other Vancouver neighbourhoods by targeting organized crime, drug dealing, drug houses, problem businesses involved in the drug trade, and improving coordination with health services and other agencies that link drug users to withdrawal management (detox), treatment, counseling and prevention services.

Source: City of Vancouver, "Four Pillars Drug Strategy," http://www.vancouver.ca/fourpillars (accessed September 23, 2010)

INSITE INTERVENTIONS, 2009	
Number of Visitors	**Type of Intervention**
702	average number of visits per day
484	overdose interventions with no fatalities
2,492	clinical treatment interventions
6,242	referrals to other social and health services; the majority for detox and addiction treatments
411	admissions to Onsite, the adjoining detox treatment facility

the area, a problem exacerbated by needle-sharing and the increasing availability of new illegal drugs. Ruth was especially supportive of the city's "four pillar" approach to grappling with substance abuse, which links harm reduction with prevention, treatment and enforcement. After discussion it was agreed that First United should work with other agencies to seek government support for a supervised injection site, although this was obviously a contentious proposal. When the process bogged down, lawyers for "Persons Living with AIDs" asked if the church would be willing to open a supervised injection site—or alternatively a mock site—to help spur government action. After Oversight Board members were briefed on the legal implications of doing it, they agreed that a mock site should open for one week in the First United building to allow the public to understand the nature of the work of a supervised injection site. In the fall of 2002 the mock site was set up in the 600-square-foot upstairs room that had served for some twenty-five years as the Outreach School. The site was designed to look as realistic as possible, with nurses in attendance whenever it was open to the public, and it received visits from members of the local community as well as from many professionals and decision makers from the wider community. But it was not until September 21, 2003, that the safe injection site called Insite opened on East Hastings Street, with the support of the City of Vancouver, the Province of British Columbia and the federal government. After seven years of operation, indications are that many lives have been saved and many more lives encouraged towards a life free of drugs.

MISSION STATEMENT

At the end of the 1990s the team at First United revamped the church's mission statement to reflect the changing nature of the ministry.

Inspired by the Christian Gospel
which nurtures, empowers, liberates,
First United Church is an inner-city ministry
of the United Church of Canada.
Called by the Spirit to be part of
the Downtown Eastside of Vancouver,
this ministry:
affirms the worth of individuals,
empowers communities, and
works for social justice.

ADVOCACY

A few weeks before the arrival of Ruth Wright in 1997, Susan Henry had joined Stephen Gray and Leslie Campbell on the advocacy team. When, three years later, health considerations caused Leslie Campbell to resign, Janet Berry became the third member of the team. The events of a "normal" day for the advocates might include going to bat for a terminal cancer patient being evicted from his low-cost housing unit; supporting a teen-aged prostitute who wanted to quit the sex trade but was unable to get social assistance because she had never held down a real job; or mediating in a child custody dispute. But periodically the advocates also had to deal with adjustments in government regulations related

First Things First published the following lament by First United advocate Susan Henry in September 1998:

The BC Government recently passed legislation limiting support services to the unemployable, the disabled and families with children.

Unemployed people who are now on income assistance and are expected to find work will receive no money for a telephone to contact employers; no money to get resumes printed, mailed or faxed; no money to take a bus to a job interview; no money for suitable work clothing; no money for glasses so they can see well enough to fill out job applications; and no money for dental work so they can look presentable enough to hire.

With this emphasis on lowering income assistance rates and benefits in order to push people into work, large numbers of people are suffering. For example, a single mother fleeing an abusive relationship is denied a crisis grant to buy a bed for her child. A bi-polar young man is denied disability benefits because his application does not fit the wording of the legislation, and he also refuses to appeal the denial because he believes "they" know what they are doing and he cannot contradict "them." A young man who has an overdue student loan but who has recently lost an arm in an industrial accident is denied income assistance—even though the federal government student loan program is going to garnishee his entire $900-a-month Worker's Compensation Benefits, leaving him penniless for nine months.

It is to help people in such situations that the advocacy program at First United Church exists.[55]

to social assistance and health-related issues, and 1997 was the year that the Guaranteed Available Income for Need (GAIN) legislation was replaced by BC Benefits. It now became much more difficult for people to qualify for social assistance or for the handicapped allowance. Further changes a few years later made it even more difficult to successfully appeal decisions that went against the applicant. Both of these government decisions meant more interventions for First United's advocates. In addition, several other churches and agencies in the Downtown Eastside were referring their most challenging advocacy requests to First United Church, because the staff had developed such a remarkable reputation for competence in this very difficult field. The team was also being called upon again to provide advocacy training for people doing similar work in other churches and agencies, something they had frequently done in the 1980s.

PROGRAMS

Several fine community workers with a variety of backgrounds and skills shared the program responsibilities from the mid-1990s through to 2007. Some, like volunteer Doree Piercy with the Give-A-Gift program, had served for twenty years or more. Susan Garnham, and later Chris Lofting, coordinated the activity programs in the gym, supported always by faithful volunteers. Linda Ostrom, who had taken the two-year community social service worker course at Douglas College, became the food and clothing coordinator in October 1996 and soon took on the additional responsibility of overseeing and training the Downtown Eastside volunteers, a group of some two dozen people from the community who helped in the kitchen or did maintenance jobs. Linda also included them as active volunteers in sorting and displaying the clothing donated to the church and in monitoring

Joan Drabek was coordinator of volunteers at First United Church from 2000 to 2005. Joan herself volunteers with the Jewish–Muslim group that provides and serves a Sunday meal to the community each month.

Sandwich-makers are busy in the kitchen of Highlands United Church in North Vancouver. Highlands is one of several churches that regularly provides food for the people sleeping at First United Church.

the clothing room, which was open for a few hours each day. In time she recommended some of them for part-time paying jobs at the church or elsewhere in the community on the strength of their volunteer work at First United.

In 1998 a young man named Don Evans began volunteering several days each month in the church office. He soon became aware of the income tax assistance volunteers provided during tax season and recruited several friends to help. The following spring they completed more than two thousand forms. In April 1999 Don became the receptionist at First United Church and during his fourteen months in that position he continued to

---

In September 1997 this plea for volunteers was printed in *First Things First:*

HOPE AND POSSIBILITY

Once upon a time there was a lonely young man. He lived in a tiny room in an inner city hotel. He was trying to leave the darkness of his past behind, so he turned a corner by choosing to avoid the friends with whom he had spent time in a haze of drugs and alcohol. As he came to know loneliness, he knew depression, and he knew how vulnerable he was to the pull of going back to the old life style.

He wandered in to First United Church and discovered a group that met on Mondays and Thursdays. He wondered if this could be a place where he could spend some time with people, have a hot meal and maybe even make some new friends.

One person he met there always noticed him and greeted him with a smile. An older man, this person was quiet and friendly. They played cribbage and chess together and chatted about everyday things. The young man found himself looking forward to seeing the older man when he came each week. He believed this new friend liked him, and during their time together he never felt lonely.

As his trust grew, the young man felt safe enough to tell his new friend some things about himself. The older man listened and although his face was serious, his eyes showed sympathy and acceptance, and he praised the young man for turning his life around. They began to talk about hope and possibility.

Family Friendship Place (Wednesday 11 a.m.–2 p.m.) and the United Circle (Monday and Thursday 11 a.m.–2 p.m.) need volunteers like the older man in this story. Could you volunteer three hours a week to be a presence in one of our programs? The benefits to everyone involved are boundless.[56]

---

organize and coordinate the income tax program, being relieved of his duties there when he was needed upstairs at the "income tax station."

Volunteer "Sparrow" washing and massaging feet. BAYNE STANLEY PHOTO

One evening in the late 1990s a new volunteer arrived at the WISH Centre carrying a large bowl, towels and several kinds of soothing oils. Her offer to provide foot care for the women at the centre was certainly appreciated. But this simple volunteer offering was to have an even greater influence in the years ahead. Some months later Margaret Elliott, a new program staff member at First United, having heard about the earlier experience at the WISH Centre, introduced a foot-care program at First United; she called it "Saving Soles." With the benefit of advice and encouragement from the nurses at the Main Street Health Clinic, this new program became a contribution to better health as well as to better sociability as it provided greater opportunities for substantial conversations with the staff or volunteers who were helping on any given day. Seeing the foot-care program in action, Bruce Cowburn, who worked on fund development at First United Church during these years, wrote:

> I was leaving the main office at the church and noticed the foot care activity for the first time. There was a client playing classical guitar on the inside Gore Avenue stairs, Margaret Elliott, her long hair flowing, on bended knee adjusting the water temperature, an

elderly gent with his feet in the soothing water. I had to stop and catch my breath and wipe the water from my eyes. This powerful vision clearly reinforced in me the mission of the church. Love and care in action.[57]

Karli Bereska, who joined the program staff team in early 2003, picked up the responsibility for foot care, and over the next several months other volunteers participated in this meaningful experience. Since 2005 volunteers have come to the church most weekday mornings to provide foot care. For the men and women of the Downtown Eastside who are often weary from walking, having their feet soaked in warm water, engaging in conversation with a friendly volunteer and then pulling on a new pair of socks is a wonderful experience.

FUND DEVELOPMENT

Fundraising remained a constant challenge at First United during the 1997/2007 decade, and in 1998 Bruce Cowburn was contracted to coordinate fund development on a part-time basis. One of the projects during this period was a booklet called *First: A Ministry of Caring*, published in June 1999 to call attention to the ministry's financial needs. A contributor to the booklet was Dr. Lois Yelland, Vancouver District medical health officer, who wrote this appreciation of First United's programs and advocacy team:

> I strongly applaud the way in which First United Church has responded to the needs of Vancouver's Downtown Eastside. It has created a safe and caring haven in the midst of so much suffering and despair for hundreds of people each day. The services offered address many needs—physical, psychological, emotional and spiritual—and many issues—violence, substance abuse, literacy, poverty, homelessness and mental illness. The nurturing and

non-judgmental atmosphere makes it a place where everyone feels welcome. It is little wonder then that the numbers seeking refuge have doubled over the past few years.[58]

Another fundraising project during these years involved the former United Church mission boat, the *Thomas Crosby IV*, which was built in 1922 and served the church on the Central Coast from 1937 to 1967. It was now called the *Argonaut* and since 1970 had been owned by Julian Matson, who carefully maintained it at Boat Harbour, just south of Nanaimo. I had been the missionary/captain of the *Crosby* from 1960 to 1962, and when I had learned that the ship and captain were available for charters, I suggested that we could use it for a fundraising project. First United then chartered the *Argonaut* for a week, and we arranged a series of four-hour excursions from a base in North Vancouver.

The Safeway store at Broadway and Commercial designated First United Church as its charity for support by customers in the winter of 2006–2007. Here the area member of Parliament, Libby Davies, stands with Marion Young, Amanda Trimble, Ruth Wright and the store manager.

Daily morning worship in the sanctuary at First United Church, Vancouver, in 2003.

Each cruise, which included a gourmet lunch or dinner and a cruise up Indian Arm, carried twenty paying guests and three of the *Crosby*'s former missionary-skippers, who took turns being available to tell stories of the days when this special ship had served the United Church. This project raised $12,000 for First United.

In May 2001 another successful fundraising project was a benefit concert, presented by the Vancouver Welsh Men's Choir at Shaughnessy Heights United Church. The church was packed and $8,000 was raised for First United. But financing all of the church's programs remained a continuing problem, and in the fall of 2005 the church faced a funding crisis. Donations and bequests were simply not keeping up to the increased operation costs. At this point Ruth Wright was interviewed by a *Vancouver Sun* reporter for a high-profile article that appeared in the paper in November. As a direct result of that article, new First United supporters donated $40,000. Once again the immediate crisis had been averted. And once again First United was made aware that when the mission's story is told, the wider community does respond.

THE CONGREGATION

In the summer of 1998 the Very Reverend Bob Smith retired. Looking back on his time at First United, he later wrote:

> "Preach the gospel to every creature—and if necessary, use words." That admonition was uttered eight hundred years ago by St. Francis of Assisi, but it might very well have been written last week as the mission statement of First United Church. Day after day, year after year volunteers and staff members present the gospel in the form of soup, dry socks, life-changing phone calls, a clean towel, a homely truth, a hug, a bus ticket home, a safe, warm place to sleep, a friendly grin. And day after day, and year after year—when it is necessary and appropriate—the volunteers and staff use words, saying to the despised and rejected in the name of Jesus, "You are not a piece of junk. You are a beloved forgiven child of God. And we are here to walk with you as you reach out for that new life which God in Christ wills for you." [59]

In the year that followed Bob Smith's retirement, responsibility for leadership in the congregation was shared by several staff members and volunteers. Then in 1999 the Reverend Brian Burke was called to have primary responsibility for the congregation

The Reverend Brian Burke stands in the sanctuary of First United. BAYNE STANLEY PHOTO

Brian Burke was born in Montreal in 1946 but his family moved to Vancouver when he was six years old. As his family was Roman Catholic, he attended Vancouver College for his high school then went on to the University of BC where he earned a BA and his teaching certificate. However, he only taught for one year before going to Ottawa in 1969 to work in the office of Prime Minister Pierre Trudeau. In 1973 he began work in the national office of the NDP and later in the Ottawa offices of Ian Waddell (three years) and Margaret Mitchell (one year).

Brian then returned to Vancouver, and in 1991 while studying theology at the Vancouver School of Theology in preparation for ordained ministry, he was an intern at First United Church. He also served as a part-time student minister at South Hill and Wilson Heights churches in Vancouver. Brian was ordained in 1996 and served a three-point pastoral charge in southeastern Saskatchewan for three years prior to his call to First United Church in 1999.

Huddy Roddan, Reverend Philip Cable and Esther (Roddan) Carter.

and also to provide pastoral care to the mission. Brian listened well, had a big heart, and was a much appreciated friend to many, many people, both from the congregation and from the wider Downtown Eastside community. He gave considerable time and leadership to the Dugout Drop-In Centre and other inter-agency programs that addressed serious community problems. However, in July 2003 Brian left to become minister of St. John's United Church in Vancouver's West End.

Growing uncertainty about the long-term future of the congregation at First United

Philip Cable was born in 1956 and raised in Cobourg, Ontario. He attended the University of Guelph where he received a Bachelor of Science in Agriculture in 1979. He became a candidate for ministry in 1984, graduated from Queen's Theological College and was ordained in 1988. His first ministry was in Newtown–Waterford, New Brunswick. He then took special training in counselling and worked as a hospital chaplain in and near Halifax for six years. In 1997 he came to British Columbia as minister of St. Paul's United Church in Burnaby and soon afterward became a member of the First United Oversight Board. In 2000 he moved to Mount Seymour United in North Vancouver and in 2003 became con-gregational minister at First United Church.

resulted in a decision by the congregation and presbytery that the vacancy caused by Brian Burke's departure would be filled by a term appointment, rather than a "call" without a time limit. As a result, the Reverend Philip Cable, minister at Mount Seymour United Church in North Vancouver, was appointed for a two-year term as minister of the congregation and a member of the mission team.

In 2005 the Reverend Maggie Watts-Hammond became a year-long intern, and she later described that experience as "life-changing." This was not unexpected; through the years many of the interns had discovered that, when they least expected it, God's Spirit would break through and bless them, and Maggie had spoken to others who had reacted to the interning experience in this way. They had told her that "we have been formed by the place and the people. The Spirit leaps out at you in unexpected places." In a recent conversation she gave an account of an unforgettable experience near the front door of First United Church.

I was standing near the open door at the Hastings Street entrance. At the foot of the steps there was a very drunk woman in a wheel chair. The man pushing her chair was equally drunk. The woman looked up at me and shouted, "Hey, preacher lady, come and give

us a blessing!" I proceeded down the steps and gave them a blessing. When I finished, the woman said to me, "Now I will bless you."
And she did![60]

The people of the First United congregation and in the wider Downtown Eastside community are full of surprises and
blessings.

Ruth Wright went on a sabbatical leave in 2004–2005 and
her position was filled by the Reverend Rose-Hannah Gaskin,
a former psychiatric nurse, who had served as a minister in rural Cape Breton and as part of the team at St. Andrew's-Wesley
United Church in Vancouver's West End. Her leadership was
much appreciated by the staff and community members, and the
Oversight Board benefited from her observations and analysis
of the mission. On her initiative a video was developed featuring
interviews with many of the men and women who had been part
of First United during the previous two generations.

Following her sabbatical year, Ruth immersed herself again in
the life of the mission, speaking about the work of First United to
congregations throughout the Lower Mainland and Vancouver
Island. She also participated in challenging committee work at
the national level. Then in September 2006 she submitted her
resignation, to take effect June 30, 2007, by which date she would
have completed a full ten years at First United. During that time
she provided strong leadership both locally and on national
committees. As First United Church's first female lead minister,
she had developed particularly effective working relationships
with many of the agencies committed to the needs of women in
the community. Her work and that of her community team had
been recognized by the YMCA with a Power of Peace Award in
2005. The citation reads:

With the Reverend Ruth Wright, superintendent of this United

Church of Canada Mission, the members of the First United community team play a crucial part in the heart of Vancouver's Downtown Eastside. Whether as volunteers, advocates, programmers, street ministers, cooks or in other front-line roles, they reach out from the corner of Gore and East Hastings for justice, social change and a better existence for all. Their inner-city programs welcome and support all community members, especially those experiencing issues such as poverty, violence, discrimination, disability, racism, addiction and hunger in their everyday lives.

For many years the Vancouver Burrard Presbytery and the First United Oversight Board had been considering the viability of maintaining the small congregation that gathered each Sunday morning at the church at Gore and East Hastings. By 2007 there were, in fact, so few members that it was difficult to secure enough people to chair the required committees and carry the administrative responsibilities of a congregation. The Oversight Board was especially concerned about the budget requirement for an ordained minister on a half-time basis. After members of the congregation were given opportunities to express their concerns to representatives of both the Oversight Board and the Vancouver Burrard Presbytery, they decided to dissolve, effective June 30, 2007. The work of First United Church would continue; the Sunday morning church service would not.

The Reverend Don Robertson, chair of the Oversight Board from 2006 to 2008.

Jim Cryder, chair of the Oversight Board at First United Church from 2008 to 2010.

The dissolution of the congregation was timed to coincide with Ruth Wright's departure and the end date of the Reverend Philip Cable's second two-year contract. Now the Oversight Board, in consultation with the presbytery, embarked on a major review of future ministry leadership requirements, and as happens with any congregation going through a change of ministers, a joint needs assessment was undertaken by a committee that included representation from the presbytery and from the church. This process consumed several months of the time and energy of the board chair, Don Robertson, and other board members, but they gave it generously, knowing that their final report would have a great influence on the future direction of First United Church.

Over the years the Oversight Board has been given amazing leadership by men and women who truly care about the ministry of First United Church. After the many years of Jim Hillson's tenure as chair of the board, new leaders offered their time and cnergy. Geoff Wilkins, Ian Housego and Pat Burns each served as chair for several years. They were followed by Don Robertson, under whose inspiring leadership the Oversight Board addressed the challenge of reshaping the mission of First United Church as new ministry staff were being sought in 2007. The current chair (2010) is Jim Cryder.

═ CHAPTER 9 ═

2007 . . .

Vision for the Future

In mid-May 2007, I was asked to return to First United Church, starting on July 1, the day both Ruth Wright and Philip Cable would conclude their ministries, to be the minister there until the two vacancies were filled. After a gap of thirty-three years, it was a great privilege to be back at 320 East Hastings Street each weekday. Many things seemed much the same, especially the faithful commitment of volunteers and staff to alleviating the pain and frustration of members of the community. But many things were, of course, very different. Now there were people sleeping in the pews during the day. There was a soup line at 8:30 a.m. And there was a brief worship time each morning at 8:45 when a few of us gathered at the front of the sanctuary. This was definitely a different time and there were more changes to come.

Since the decision to dissolve the congregation, the members of the Oversight Board had been working on the difficult task of deciding First United's future. However, knowing that it might be the end of 2007 before they selected and installed a new ministry team, they needed to ensure that in that interim period the relationship with other churches and community agencies remained strong. To this end they hired Michael Clague, a former director of the neighbouring Carnegie Community Centre, as a consultant on a part-time basis. He knew the community well and had the respect and confidence of both First Church staff members and community agency leaders. Michael organized three large community workshops in May and June then brought together small groups of people from fifteen of the local churches and agencies during July and August to ask for their comments and suggestions. Out of these gatherings came the assurance that First United was still highly respected in the community; the Board also learned that the community hoped that in the future the church would not become just another agency but would continue to provide both a spiritual presence as well as the social service, advocacy and social action ministries that it had provided in the past.

The members of the Oversight Board were now free to re-imagine the role of the church and develop a vision for its future. They decided that this vision should not have a rigid framework; instead it would outline a series of steps that would lead into a new way of carrying out First United's mission. These steps also helped to make clear what First United was *not* to be:

1. We are committed to re-inventing and re-imagining a Worship Community at the heart of the mission. This will not be a "traditional congregational model"; rather it will be a fresh and different way of people coming together for prayer, study, social analysis and giving voice to issues so that health, wholeness and justice might prevail in the Downtown Eastside of Vancouver. We do not know what shape this will take. We do know the mission must be rooted in the Gospel of Jesus Christ and in

the people and the realities of the Downtown Eastside. The minister will take the lead in this exciting process of discernment and building. His/her leadership will help shape the vision.

2. We are committed to a staffing model that is new for us. It will consist of three ministries. The lead minister will be the minister of Community Life and will be responsible for the support and general oversight of the life and work of the mission. A second ministry will be in the area of program administration and program development (The Ministry of Hospitality). A third ministry is in the area of administration (The Ministry of Administration) which includes office, finances and building. All staff of the mission will relate to and be responsible to one of these persons. In the staffing model we are committed to developing collegial, collaborative working relationships. The minister of Community Life will be an ordained minister of the United Church of Canada. The other two positions may be lay or ordained and preference will be given to people active in the United Church of Canada.

3. The neighbourhood of the Downtown Eastside is changing. This requires changing initiatives and strategies for the mission. Centres of poverty and homelessness are exploding in surrounding communities such as Surrey, Langley, North Vancouver and Abbotsford. This calls for the mission of First United to consider these changes in relation to our regional role. We also realize that our present facility is close to the end of its useful life and will require major renovations or, indeed, the imagining of a different facility related to future needs.[61]

Armed with this vision for the future, the Oversight Board began interviewing candidates for the new ministry team.

Ric Matthews, Minister of the Mission and Community Life

In 2005 when Ruth Wright was on sabbatical leave, she had spent several months at the Pretoria Methodist City Mission in South Africa. While she was there, a group of twenty-two Canadian visitors, all of them associated with Shaughnessy Heights United Church in Vancouver and led by Ric and Nina Matthews, arrived to see the mission. Ric Matthews was an ordained minister of the Methodist Church in South Africa and had served for eight years as a minister in the inner city of Johannesburg. However, after leaving the ministry, he had spent fifteen years as a change management consultant, first in South Africa and then in Vancouver. In conversation with him, Ruth learned that in 2005, having become increasingly restless in the business environment, he had assumed a consulting role with World Vision, while at the same time applying to the United Church of Canada

for admission to ordained ministry. In 2007 when he was made aware of the vacancy at First United Church, he read through the description of the mission and the goals developed by the Oversight Board and submitted his application. He was selected by the Board and appointed minister of the mission and Community Life on July 10, 2007.

The Reverend Ric Matthews, minister of the mission and community life, began his lead-role ministry in August 2007.

Ric Matthews began his ministry at First United Church in August 2007, although he divided his time between World

This photograph was taken in 1991 at the first meeting of the African National Congress leadership that was held subsequent to Nelson Mandela's release and the unbanning of the ANC in February 1990. Ric Matthews attended this meeting, held at the Alpha Training Centre just outside of Johannesburg, and led a three-day trust-building workshop, on behalf of Kimberly-Clark South Africa, for enfranchised white managers and disenfranchised black workers. On extreme left is Mandla Sibeko, personal assistant to Ric in Ric's management consulting firm; second from right is Ric; and between Ric and Mandela is Arthur Mzimela, human resources manager at Kimberley-Clark.

Vision and First United until October. Now he had to learn about his new community, his work colleagues, the United Church way of functioning, and the vision for the future that the Oversight Board had developed over the past months. His education on the subject of the Downtown Eastside community was made easier because he was able to participate in some of the small group meetings that had been coordinated by social planner Michael Clague. He also used his first weeks at First United to have a substantial conversation with each of the fourteen people on the church staff as well as discussions with board members in which he presented some of his own ideas for the way ahead. He suggested that First United should be a "new kind of community in old town Vancouver," and he asked the board to approve the

Ric Matthews was born in Pretoria, South Africa, in 1953 and attended elementary school and the Victoria Boys High School there. He studied at the University of South Africa in Pretoria and at Rhodes University in Grahamstown, Eastern Cape Province. Following the Methodist tradition of serving as student and minister simultaneously (the probation period), in 1977 Ric became responsible for the leadership of two inner-city churches where he faced the harsh realities of extreme poverty, injustice, violence and apartheid. He was ordained in 1984, and three years later the Methodist Church seconded him to work in industry, focussing on redressing injustice in the workplace. This assignment led him to become a consultant to industry in South Africa, where he helped organizations to embrace change so that it served the best interests of all concerned. Of this experience he says that it was "a tremendous privilege to be able to work intentionally with factors in the workplace that prevent people from living the kind of life that the gospel intended for us."

Ric Matthews served on the Methodist Church of South Africa's Committee for Justice and Reconciliation. He also invented a board game called "Know Me," which has been used worldwide to enable conflict resolution, relationship-building and the development of understanding across racial, religious and sectarian lines. He and his family came to Vancouver in August 1997.

following as guiding principles that should be reflected in all the activities of the church:

1. The surroundings will be attractive and safe, the conduct of staff professional.
2. Interactions will be personal as each member of the community is a person with a name and feelings.
3. We will be an inclusive community. Any person from any level or sphere of life will be able to see value in participating, both as someone with something to give as well as to receive.
4. All activities will offer deliberate opportunity and encouragement to move beyond the present reality to new skills, ability, capacity, growth, greater functionality. (Developmental–Incremental)
5. In all programs and activities participants and onlookers

will be touched with hope. (Inspiring–Transformational) Real stories will be shared at a personal level in life-giving and healing ways, evoking spiritual questions and making available spiritual resources.

6. In all activities we will be eco-responsible, reducing our environmental impact, reducing waste and harnessing natural energy.

By November 2007 both board and staff had decided that the First United building needed to be made more attractive. Artist, teacher and painter Ann Thorsteinsson was engaged to refurbish the interior of the building, and she enlisted a small crew of community workers and a First Nations artist. They painted the walls and then added First Nations motifs in the entrance area, the main office and the upstairs meeting room. All the office doors were painted bright colours, and this made an immediate and enormous difference. Ann also organized three half-day workshops

Some of the art work from Ann Thorsteinsson's workshops has been mounted on the wall of the chapel.

where high school students from the North Shore joined with men and women from the Downtown Eastside community to paint seventy-five plywood panels, most of them roughly a foot by a foot and a half in size, which were then mounted on the wall of the chapel, taking up one entire side wall.

A two-day staff retreat in the first week of November provided an opportunity for Ric to learn more about his new colleagues and to explore with staff members the impact of new directions for the mission flowing from the vision of the Oversight Board and the guiding principles recently approved by the board. In line with the second guiding principle that specified personal interactions, the program staff now shifted their work patterns so that each had a clear focus on the people instead of the program. This meant that each program staff person could have a "caseload" of twenty-five to thirty people and support them as individuals, not just as members of a program group.

Over the next few months several staff changes occurred as well, all of them designed to make the work at First United more effective. Tony Weall assumed the role of administrator, contributing his extensive knowledge of information technology to redesign First United's computer networks and information databases. After Ric's arrival, I had been asked to continue in a part-time pastoral role, but in April 2008 I was also asked to assume leadership in fund development; at this time we faced a deficit of $300,000 in our annual budget. Christopher Darling became the bookkeeper in March 2008 on a part-time basis, but before long his services were required full time as the budget increased so dramatically.

When the congregation was dissolved at the end of June 2007, many had expressed the hope that some kind of mid-week service would be developed to take the place of the Sunday service, and by late November planning had been completed for the first of a series of Wednesday evening "celebrations." Invitations were sent out to the whole community to attend a "sit-down" dinner in the gym followed by an informal theme presentation in words and video. The first dinner was attended by one hundred and thirty people—all that the fire regulations will allow in the gym. Since that first dinner, every Wednesday at six p.m. there has been a lineup outside the door to the gym and the first hundred and thirty have sat down to dine. About half of them are "regulars" who seem to feel part of the First United family. The food is prepared by one of the staff cooks, supported by volunteers, and served to the tables by volunteers from other United churches throughout the city; one Wednesday of each month the servers are the members of youth groups from two of these churches. While this celebration is much like the "community at worship," Ric Matthews always seeks to create an atmosphere where people of all faiths or of no faith will feel equally welcome.

MINISTRY LEADERSHIP TEAM

With the arrival of the Reverend Sandra Severs as Minister of Hospitality and Programs on January 1, 2008, the senior staff, which included the administrator and the two full-time clergy, began to meet regularly as the Ministry Leadership Team (MLT).

Sandra Severs was born in Oshawa, Ontario, in January 1960 and attended Cannington Public School and Brock High School in her hometown of Cannington, Ontario. She earned a Bachelor of Environmental Studies at the University of Waterloo and an MDiv degree from Emmanuel College, Victoria University. She was ordained in May 1987 and settled in the Northminster pastoral charge in southern Alberta until 1991. Graduate studies at the University of Calgary brought her an MA in Environmental Ethics in 1993.

In 1992 Sandra Severs was called with her spouse, the Reverend Don Collett, to Springbank United Church in the Foothills Presbytery in Alberta, where they job-shared until 1998. They moved to the North Shore of Vancouver in 1998. Sandra chaired the national Interchurch Interfaith Committee of the United Church of Canada during major studies on Jewish-Christian and Muslim-Christian relations, and she was chair of Vancouver–Burrard Presbytery from 2008 to 2010.

Within the next few months, Ric Matthews also developed what is sometimes referred to as an advisory council—a small group of community members who meet with him one morning each week to provide advice and support. In this forum the members are encouraged to give honest feedback about what is happening around the church. While it is appreciated by the people who are part of it, Ric also values it highly because the exposure enriches his knowledge of the community.

The Emerging Vision

Throughout 2008 the Ministry Leadership Team and the Oversight Board continued to develop a working strategy for the future ministry at First United. It included the mission statement of First United Church as well as a new identity statement.

IDENTITY STATEMENT (WHO WE ARE)

As an inner-city mission of the United Church of Canada that has been called to be a part of the Vancouver Downtown Eastside, we seek to be and become a faithful and authentic "Gospel Community," which, rooted in our Christian faith, is:

Inclusive of all people regardless of their place of residence, religious or political beliefs, economic or social circumstances.

Grounded in the call to be both "Christ for others" and "recognize Christ in others," valuing diversity and individual difference and living out a relationship of mutuality.

Intentional in its primary commitment to stand with and to sit at table with those who otherwise live on the margins of society.

Inspirational in celebrating life, in proactively fostering peace and justice, and in consciously and actively embracing responsibility for the environment.

The community of faith, which is this First United Church

mission, will strive to include people of various economic means, youth and children while always remaining rooted in standing with those who are exiled in their own land.

A PLACE OF REFUGE, 24–7

At ten o'clock on the evening of Sunday, December 7, 2008, Ric Matthews picked up his home phone to hear, "Hi, Ric. It's Gregor Robertson. Tomorrow I will be inaugurated as mayor, and I've been meeting with a team of advisors for several hours, looking for ways to address the needs of the homeless. In the group here are Janice Abbot, executive director at Atira Women's Shelters, and Judy Graves, the housing advocate for

---

SIX MEANINGFUL GREEK WORDS

Ric Matthews suggests that both the identity and mission statements are anchored in six Greek words that defined the early church: *kairos, ekklesia, kerygma, koinonia, didache* and *diakonia*. These words mean:

Kairos—God's window of opportunity, the fullness of time, the sacred carpe diem.

Ekklesia—the people of God, a community in which God is encountered and celebrated. Being Church is about being one in the Spirit, it is about the way we live with each other, our neighbours and the earth.

Kerygma—Proclamation, preaching, the encounter with God and with the Gospel. Being Church is encountering the sacred in ourselves and in others.

Koinonia—Fellowship, community, partnership, hospitality. We believe that Being Church is about discovering life-giving personal validation, belonging and interdependence.

Didache—Teaching, learning, discovering new insights and understanding. Being Church is about reaching for and being helped to attain healing, growth and wholeness. It is about freeing the potential that exists within us individually and collectively.

Diakonia—Service, outreach, caring, making a difference. Being Church is about seeing and meeting the basic needs of others, about working for justice and peace. It is about being physically and emotionally in the places of brokenness and about challenging in actions and words the systemic drivers and sustainers of injustice. Specifically, it includes authentic critique and prophetic challenge of social, economic and political policies and practices.

Some of the 250 homeless people sleeping on the pews and on the floor in the sanctuary at First United Church in 2009.

the City of Vancouver. We've confronted the fact that we have an urgent need that we have to act on immediately. We know that you currently have up to a hundred people sleeping on your church pews from eight-thirty in the morning until four in the afternoon, Monday through Friday. I am calling to ask if you could extend that service."

"By how much?" Ric asked.

"To every night of the week," the mayor-elect said.

Ric agreed to explore this request with staff and get back to him the following day.

By eleven on Monday night it had been settled that First United would be open during the day from Monday to Friday plus seven nights a week. It was also agreed that up to a hundred and fifty people would be sleeping overnight in the church. On December 15, just as Vancouver's coldest winter in many years was beginning, First United accommodated overnight guests for the first time. On several nights in that bitterly cold month there were more than three hundred people sleeping on the church's

Recently, Ric Matthews wrote the following piece, titled "First United, Desmond Tutu and Nelson Mandela: Connected by a Common Spirit and the Spirit of *ubuntu*," about the spirit that motivates him:

> In South Africa during 1977 and 1978 the Central Methodist Mission and the Anglican congregation of St. Mary's Cathedral frequently partnered in ministry within downtown central Johannesburg. As a result, I as a young minister on the Methodist staff team was privileged to work alongside Desmond Tutu, who was then the Dean of St. Mary's. It was from him that I first learned of the Zulu word *ubuntu*. Since then he has frequently spoken and written about this critical concept, one that captures the core philosophy at the base of the miraculously peaceful transformation of the socio-political landscape of South Africa. It is also a philosophy so powerfully reflected in the life and work of Nelson Mandela, another icon of our time whom I was privileged to meet and speak with. My own life has been profoundly impacted by these two men and the spirit of *ubuntu* that beats in their hearts.
>
> *Ubuntu* declares that a person is a person through other people, that one is only fully human when all others are also fully human, that my humanity is fundamentally grounded in your humanity, that when one person is in pain we are all in pain and when one person celebrates we all celebrate. *Ubuntu* explains why the oppressor and the oppressed are equally dehumanized, and why in our capitalist society both winners and losers in the pursuit of power and wealth are equally dehumanized.
>
> *Ubuntu* is one of the rich cultural mores that sets free the ancient gospel truth that we are made one in Christ; that we are one body with many indispensable parts (Rom 12 and 1 Cor 12); that it is in the everyday encounters and ordinary relationships that we meet the sacred in ourselves, in others and in the space between and beyond us (Matt 25); that fullness of life is found in the interdependence and mutuality between those with power and those without, those with wealth and those without, those at the centre of mainstream society and those at the extreme margins (Gal 3).
>
> This is the truth that has characterized the community at First United for one hundred and twenty-five years. It is the truth that shapes us still today. Our past has produced a platform from which our vision for the future will take off, flying to the tomorrows on wings that are lifted by the spirit of *ubuntu* and are empowered by the Spirit that makes us one creation. It is *ubuntu* that connects us with Desmond Tutu and Nelson Mandela. It is *ubuntu* that ties together our future and our past.[62]

pews and on the floor, and the average for the first four months was two hundred and fifty per night.

For the first few weeks this refuge/shelter was funded by a partnership of the Vancouver area United Churches, the City of Vancouver, the Streetohome Foundation and the BC Housing Corporation, with all of them sharing the cost of providing the required additional staff. In mid-February BC Housing assumed full financial responsibility but also required that three hot meals be provided each day for two hundred people. By the end of February the church was open twenty-four hours a day, although guests were asked to vacate the sleeping area from five until six in the evening so that it could be cleaned. First United Church continued to pay for the unfunded expenses related to

---

Ric Matthews tells this story about how simple acts of reaching out to others can have a profound effect on both the one who makes the gesture and the one who receives:

> When Sandra Severs, minister for hospitality and program at First United, walked across Hastings Street one wet and uncomfortable morning, she was seeking the solace of a brand-name coffee. But on the street she saw a young woman doing what the local folk call the "Hastings Street shuffle"—a disturbing jerky walk with arms flailing and the body contorting, a walk induced by crack cocaine. Sandra also saw a male photographer intrusively snapping provocative images of this object of curiosity. Intervening, she gently but firmly asked the photographer to stop, despite indications from the somewhat incoherent woman that she had given permission for him to take the pictures. As the man left, the woman for a brief moment stopped her dramatic movements, the intensity about her subsided, and she stepped gently towards Sandra to engage her in a deeply authentic hug. In the sacred space of that embrace she whispered just two words: "Thank you." They stood like that for a while, then the young woman let go and staggered off down the sidewalk. But for a life-giving moment time had stood still. The woman's body was relaxed, her mind peaceful. Sanity and wholeness had broken through the darkness. And two women were each deeply and fully human. It was a precious gift that both women gave and both received. It was about *ubuntu*. It was about the gospel. It was about the truth at the centre of First United's life.[63]

Bernie Williams, master carver and the first female apprentice under the late Bill Reid, joined our host/security staff in the summer of 2009. Would it be possible, she asked, to find a place in the church for her partially completed fifteen-foot totem pole? The necessary arrangements were made and for the next two months the pole rested in the First United parking area, often surrounded by several carvers and painters at the same time. It was completed in January, and on Saturday, January 30, it was raised and dedicated and now stands in a prominent place in the northeast corner of the gym. We are grateful to Bernie and the fourteen other people who worked on the pole under her guidance.

keeping the building warm and safe twenty-four hours a day.

In February 2009, Don Evans became director of administration at First United. Ten years earlier Don had worked as the receptionist at the church and had been an active volunteer prior to that. He now brought his enormous energy and passion to his new role with the senior staff. One of his first tasks was to create a thrift store to deal with the used clothing operation, which had become unmanageable. Community volunteers sorted the clothing and other materials donated to the church,

The People's Totem Pole, created by Bernie Williams (Skundaal) with help and support from fourteen carvers and community members, was dedicated in a ceremony on January 30, 2010.

then the clothing was placed on racks in the large gallery of the church and for a few hours each day community members were free to select the clothes they needed. There were three serious problems with the system. First, valuable program staff time was being spent on coordinating the volunteers. Second, there was not enough space to adequately store the unsorted boxes, and when the sorting was completed, almost half of the donations were in such bad condition that they had to be hauled away to the dump at substantial cost. Third, the area where the clothing was hung for distribution had to be a secured space. By early 2009 it was clear that using such large areas of the church for a used clothing operation that was not working was very inefficient. The solution was the leasing and renovating of a storefront on Hastings Street, forty yards east of the church entrance. All clothing was sent there for sorting, and only the items needed for the church's emergency clothing room were sent back to the church. With a store manager, a part-time staff and several volunteers, the thrift store could provide an attractive low-cost clothing outlet for the community while church program staff were released to conduct programs again. The store continues to provide employment for a few people from the community, and hundreds of individuals and families appreciate the opportunity to get good quality materials at very low cost.

Throughout 2009 the refuge operation dominated First United's agenda. Up to twenty-five host/security staff had to be hired, trained and supervised. Scores of new volunteers arrived, eager to help with the refuge, especially in the colder winter months. At the same time, the number wanting to use the showers increased tenfold, and the number of people seeking the help of advocates doubled. Since our front door was now open throughout the night, there were some occasions that required a call for the ambulance or police, and whenever security staff didn't know what to do in such an emergency, the bedside phone of one of the ministry leadership team members would ring. So it was that in the early summer it was decided that shift supervisors were necessary during the evening and night shifts to better respond to emergencies. This certainly helped but wasn't enough. In October the Board approved a new staff position: a director of operations to coordinate and supervise all of the program and refuge staff. Gillian Rhodes brought to this position several years in human resources and project management positions, most recently five years with Telus. Together with a loyal team of shift supervisors and host security staff, she brought efficiency and caring, stability and calmness to what was a very challenging environment.

When Stephen Gray became an advocate at First Church in 1991, he took a special interest in the First United Church Social Housing Society, and during 2009 he became a member of the Ministry Leadership Team with special responsibility for housing.

By October 2009 the Ministry Leadership Team included:

The Reverend Ric Matthews, minister of Mission and Community Life
The Reverend Sandra Severs, minister of Hospitality and Program
Don Evans, director of Administration
The Reverend Bob Burrows, director of Fund Development
Tony Weall, now director of Social Enterprise
Stephen Gray, director of Housing
Gillian Rhodes, director of Operations

One of the most difficult challenges for homeless people is keeping their belongings safe. Indeed, many men and women of the Downtown Eastside carried all their belongings with them all the time because there was no place in the downtown area where they could leave anything and expect to find it when they came back. Don Evans, Sandra Severs and Ric Matthews persuaded the City of Vancouver to sponsor a safe storage place at First United Church. The city agreed to a six-month trial period, provided money for the construction costs, the purchase of large plastic storage bins, and staff wages for ten hours each day. A small section of the First United parking lot was used, walls and shelving were quickly built and within a very few weeks two hundred and five storage bins were in use. Additional space was created in April 2010 to accommodate grocery carts and wheeled suitcases. This service made a huge difference in the lives of hundreds of community members.

Two other major projects emerged from the challenge of having two hundred and fifty people sleeping in the church every night. First, the men and women were sleeping on hard wooden church pews or on the floor. Second, although the women's washrooms and showers were adequate for the number of women who slept in the church, there was a desperate need for more washroom and toilet spaces for men.

Don Evans gave leadership on both projects. First United Church needed sturdy bunk beds with high quality mattresses that would resist bed bugs, but the cost of a double bunk with mattress was $500. When the need was written up in the local press, several people quickly responded with $500 donations.

Bunks at First United, which began to replace the pews in 2009.

However, the problem was not completely resolved until the provincial minister of Housing learned about the bunk-bed project and, despite the provincial budget deficit, provided the funds to obtain one hundred double bunks. All these beds were made available to both men and women, but women were able to sleep in a "women only" room if they chose. Now all that remained was the men's washroom, shower and toilet problem. More of each were urgently needed but they were all expensive. Then the City of Vancouver, BC Housing, private foundations and corporate donations provided the funds to expand the men's washrooms and provide shower space for four people.

SANCTUARY

In the late summer of 2009 a citizens' support group asked First United Church to provide sanctuary for Rodney Watson, a thirty-one-year-old American citizen facing deportation and almost certain court martial when returned to the United States. After much careful and prayerful consideration, the Oversight Board and the Ministry Leadership Team agreed to give him sanctuary. Rodney had enlisted in the US army and was assigned as a cook for a twelve-month tour of duty in Iraq. In fact, his actual assignment never involved cooking and he was forced to carry and use a gun, frequently raising the weapon against civilians. Back home in the US in 2006, shortly before the end of his three-year contract, the army ordered him to serve another three years. He chose to come to Canada and applied for admission as a refugee. He now has a wife and young son in Vancouver, and up to July 2010 there had been no reply to his latest request for a hearing on compassionate and humanitarian grounds.

FUND DEVELOPMENT

First United Church is supported by individuals, congregations, charitable foundations and corporations small and large, but the increasing number of programs and services that the mission was providing was putting more and more pressure on the budget and on the fund development team. Fortunately, just at this time several fundraising projects brought new and immediate financial support.

In the spring of 2006 the Reverend Philip Cable had spearheaded a "Miles for Mission" project in conjunction with the Vancouver marathon event and with walkers and runners sponsored by friends and relatives, raised over $40,000 for the mission. But the next two years were not as successful, and in 2009 the fund development team switched to become allied with the *Vancouver Sun* Run. Jenn Cunnings, a youth minister at St. Andrew's-Wesley United Church, volunteered to coordinate a Run/Walk for the Homeless event, and her enthusiasm and hard work helped to raise a total of $60,000 in 2009 and 2010.

In May 2008 First United Church held its first "Golf Fore the

Homeless" tournament at the University Golf Course. Eighty-four golfers signed up and the church netted $50,000, largely due to the substantial donations and sponsorships of several non-golfers. In May 2009, 102 golfers participated in the second golf tournament and we raised $30,000; 114 signed up for the third tournament and we raised $35,000. Both the golf tournaments and the Run/Walk for the Homeless events are important for reasons other than the immediate fundraising:

John Cashore celebrates a great putt at the third annual "Golf Fore The Homeless" fundraising golf tournament in May 2010.

people who have never had any connection to the work of First United Church hear stories about the need and meet people who were deeply involved. And new friends are made.

In March 2009 Laverne Gfroerer and Jacqueline Forbes-Roberts came to First United with a proposal to produce a CD that included music from classical to jazz, spirituals to blues. With it would be a twenty-four-page booklet called "A Time to Heal: Moving Beyond Homelessness" that would tell some of the story of homelessness in different parts

In 2009 First United Church sponsored a CD of music by local musicians, spearheaded by Laverne Gfroerer and Jacqueline Forbes-Roberts, called "A Time to Heal: Moving Beyond Homelessness." It was created to raise awareness of homelessness across Canada and provide a resource for groups working with the homeless to raise funds for their work.

of Canada. It was the two women's hope that groups working with the homeless would sell the CD and raise funds for their own causes. The musicians, including the Wind Quintet of the National Arts Centre Orchestra in Ottawa and some of the finest singers in Vancouver, were already committed and studio recording time was booked. Five of the twenty tracks were donated, and local musician Larry Nickel had arranged or composed twelve of the remaining fifteen. These included "Come Unto Me," which he wrote in 1969, with the violin solo played by Pinchas Zukerman.

With the help of generous friends who sponsored the production costs, First United Church teamed up with Laverne Gfroerer and Jacqueline Forbes-Roberts to produce the CD, and the local musicians featured on it performed their songs at a launching concert on October 14 that attracted an audience of eight hundred to St. Andrew's-Wesley Church. This concert was jointly sponsored by the St. Andrew's-Wesley committee called End Homelessness Now. By the beginning of 2010 almost four thousand copies had been sold, and it is hoped that Canada-wide sales will continue for some time, sales that benefit both the local marketing group and First United Church.

One month after the CD launch concert, St. Andrew's-Wesley

"Jimmy" Kinistino was a volunteer, musician and sometime resident of the First United Church shelter in 2009 and 2010. ROBERT FORBES PHOTO

United Church was filled for another concert in support of First United. Local gospel and jazz singer Dee Daniels led a team of musicians in presenting "The Sacred Music of Duke Ellington," music that had never been previously performed in Western Canada. Once again production costs were covered by donations from sponsors, and the event raised almost $40,000 for the mission.

Continuing the "Porridge Breakfast" tradition started by David Jiles twenty-three years earlier, just before the start of the Christmas rush in 2009 two successful breakfasts were held to raise funds for First United Church. The hosts invited friends, neighbours and relatives to breakfast, indicating on the invitation that the guests were encouraged to make a donation to First United.

But not all of First United's supporters are adults. One of our youngest donors, Hannah Newbury, is from Wilson Heights United Church. When she first came to a celebration service, she was eight years old, but she had been collecting pennies for many months, wanting to do something for the homeless people in our community. She brought cookies for all the people at the dinner and a modest cash donation, and then a few months later she organized all the children in her class at school to collect hundreds of pairs of socks for

Robert Milton and Hannah Newbury with an Olympic Torch. Robert is a member of the First United community and in February 2010, he was the proud bearer of the Olympic torch in the Downtown Eastside and Strathcona communities. For three years Hannah collected pennies to help the homeless, and with her school friends she has collected socks and food for the mission.

Noel MacDonald, photographer and tireless volunteer at First United, tells the story of one of his first encounters with the church at Hastings and Gore. In the fall of 2008 he and two other photographers, Wayne Kaulbach and Adam Blasberg, were looking for a project for themselves, and they approached First United with the idea of creating portraits of people from the community to add to the church's existing Christmas card program.

Wayne, Adam and I made up the criteria and process as we went along, not knowing whether we would get any uptake from the community at all. In the end, over four weeks of shooting, we photographed almost two hundred folk.

The paybacks were huge and unexpected. Community members got as much from the process as the product. They had thirty to forty-five minutes where someone really looked at them, focussing on positive features, where they had an opportunity to talk about their lives, and where we created an image that excluded their physical surrounding and showed who they were inside. Each of the three of us came away from our experience convinced that we had got significantly more than we had given. We had met funny, engaging, thoughtful people who shared their stories of community, hope, despair and victory. And the connection with those people has grown outside the project.

Over the past two years [2008–2010] we have portrayed over five hundred wonderful people. The images we created reconnected families, were gifts for special friends on the street and, for eight people, were used at their own memorial services.

It would have been a wonderful thing if that's all that happened. But I found myself drawn into the rich and vital community at Hastings and Gore. Shortly after beginning the project I started helping out in the kitchen, and that led to developing great friendships with staff and community members. I found myself realizing that my time at First United was intensely selfish. My commitment to the community was mirrored by a great gift from the First United family. I was given trust, humour, compassion and honesty from people that I call my friends. I came to learn the ebb and flow of life at First United, and I found that attentiveness, compassion and humour could break down just about any barrier.

I had a woman ask me one afternoon, "What do you do here anyway?" And it's certainly complicated. In the last few weeks I've helped serve over six hundred breakfasts on the day before welfare cheques were issued, I've handed out rigs, I've gone with my twelve-year-old son and several community members to an Olympic hockey game, I've sat with a drug-sick sixteen-year-old girl as she wept about where her life had taken her, I've held my friend Phillip's elbow as he left to go to a treatment house, and I've shared jokes with dozens of my pals. And occasionally I pick up my camera.

So what do I do? I open my mind and my heart to receive a gift that can only come from loving and being loved.[64]

the homeless. On Valentine's Day 2010, Hannah brought special treats for the community members again.

THE 2010 OLYMPICS AND THE DOWNTOWN EASTSIDE

In the run-up to the 2010 Olympic Winter Games in Vancouver, there were dire predictions of a government attempt to "clean up" the Downtown Eastside, as had happened before Expo 86. But no such attempt was made prior to the Games. In fact, community members benefited when large television sets were donated to First United, the Dugout and other Downtown Eastside agencies so that local people could watch the games and enjoy television into the future. Still, the Games did nothing to mitigate the homelessness in the community.

As a result, First United initiated a "Share the Gold" campaign—thousands of people waving gold scarves at the Games—to raise awareness of homelessness locally and—through the

First Church community members with Share the Gold scarves spread the message at an Olympic curling game in 2010.

media surrounding the Games—nationally and internationally. By creating a sea of yellow-gold during the games, it was hoped that people might hear the call to harness the energy, resources and goodwill that had made the Games a success for the challenging work ahead to eradicate homelessness by 2015.

In late November 2009 forty representatives of churches, political organizations and community leaders attended a meeting at First United Church to consider the Share the Gold possibility, and strong endorsement from this group encouraged First United to continue the project. On February 3, 2010, just nine days before the opening ceremony for the Winter Olympics, a hundred and fifty people attended a panel discussion at First United to hear MLA Shane Simpson, MLA Jenny Kwan, Mayor Gregor Robertson, MP Libby Davies and the leader of those opposed to the Olympics, Dr. Chris Shaw. Despite their differing views on the Games, all the panelists supported the concept of "Share the Gold."

Robert Milton is a talented soccer player from the Git'Ksan territory in northern BC, but he is also an active member of our community, and we were all pleased when he was chosen to carry the Olympic torch through the Downtown Eastside on February 12, 2010. A couple of days later the Reverend Sandra Severs heard music outside her window, and when she investigated, she saw Robert, wearing his Olympic jacket and holding the torch, standing on the street. Beside him stood another Native man singing a First Nations song. It seemed apparent to Sandra that the man did not know Robert personally but was just thrilled that he had been one of the torchbearers. Having the torch relay pass through our community had really meant a lot to the Downtown Eastside residents.

THE HOPE LIVES HERE INITIATIVE

In 2008 the Ministry Leadership Team, the Oversight Board and special consultants began discussing a plan to redevelop the church property at Gore and Hastings to provide more housing for the community. But the goal this time was to provide more than just shelter; it was to provide shelter in the context of community, because homelessness, addiction and poverty all have their roots in a desolation of the spirit—an absence of a sense of belonging, acceptance and validation. The goal was to create a new kind of church community. This plan came to be called the "Hope Lives Here Initiative."

The Reverend Sandra Severs, who leads this project at First United, says that the Hope Lives Here Initiative is "just an extension of what we've been doing." What is clear to her and to the Leadership Team and the Oversight Board is that First United has embraced the challenge of being a church at the margins of society. What is not clear, but is part of the emerging future, is what the Christian church looks like when it is truly anchored at the margins of society and when it is truly inclusive of all strata in society, even different faith perspectives.

While the provincial government and the City of Vancouver have both made real progress in recent months toward addressing homelessness, the needs remain overwhelming. There is no simple solution, but the Leadership Team of First United believes there are three basic imperatives:

1. The recognition that homelessness is about belonging and "feeling at home." It's about having a place where one feels safe, where one's possessions are stored, and where one is a full and interdependent member of the family or community. To just construct new buildings—even when they are supported with professional services—does not in itself combat the alienation, dislocation, and broken relationships that underlie life at the margins of society.
2. The provision of housing that spans the whole spectrum of needs—a place of refuge for those most angry with and mistrustful of society, supportive housing for those

in treatment, supported housing for those who will need long-term support, and affordable housing for those who just need a place they can afford.

3. The provision of housing within the larger context of poverty, addiction, mental illness and a sense of despair. We urgently need a comprehensive and integrated approach across ministries such as Welfare, Health, and Housing and across all the different initiatives already on the ground.

By the end of 2009 the First United Church Housing Society, with its three buildings and 187 units, was fully integrated with the work and management of the church. Closer ties were also established with the Dugout Drop-In Centre Society and its sponsorship of a daily AA meeting. At the same time extensive new relationships were forged that will likely produce new partnerships with other institutions and government departments and ongoing collaborative efforts were established with other faith communities.

First United's goal now is to move from mainly standing alongside people in distress to walking with them to wholeness. Community members, residents of the Housing Society buildings and visitors to First United are receiving critical assistance in exploring and engaging more creative alternatives for addressing their personal challenges. The skilled team of ten community workers—including the advocates and reception services—now supplement the personal therapy provided by the onsite family therapist with numerous ongoing small groups focussed on healing and growth. Extensive support is also offered to those at risk of losing their housing. There are real people in real need right now and an urgent requirement for bold and courageous leadership.

At the end of April 2010 First United Church issued the following statement about the Hope Lives Here Initiative:

> In this 125th year of First United's presence in the Downtown Eastside, and as our part in responding to the need for bold leadership, we are today announcing a commitment to a $31-million redevelopment on our site at the corner of East Hastings Street and Gore Avenue. On that strategic corner, joining Chinatown, Strathcona and the Downtown Eastside, we will build a facility that invites and includes people from all walks of life while intentionally meeting the needs of those at the margins of society. The building will provide a wide range of housing: facilities for medical, dental and basic health care; attractions for children and families; space for reflection, prayer and celebration; areas for advocacy and counseling; and rooms for classroom learning, art and music. But this is not about providing housing or services. It is about building an inclusive community in which we encounter the sacred within us and beyond us, in which we grow into our full potential individually and collectively, in which we enjoy a deep sense of belonging and of mutual interdependence, and in which we constantly strive for justice and wholeness. The United Church of Canada has provided us with an initial $6 million in land and capital.
>
> This is a neighbourhood that speaks of human suffering, and it is a neighbourhood that sings of hope. It is where Vancouver was born and is now where we will together define the future of our city and province. With creative and courageous leadership we can not only address the challenges of homelessness, but we can free the spirit at the centre of this community and see on these streets not despair but a beacon of hope.

⇒ AFTERWORD ⇐

Are You Still a Church?

First United Church moves forward looking very different than it did fifty, ten or even five years ago, and in the absence of a Sunday morning congregation, people ask the question: "Are you still a church?" Ric Matthews has a very emphatic response to this question. He says: "We are and will remain a church! The generally accepted five marks of the church as a faith community are very clear. Church is about:

1. encountering God within the activities of that faith community
2. actively belonging to that community
3. participating in learning and growth towards wholeness
4. reaching out to meet one another's needs and working for justice
5. embracing a liturgy or visible ordered structure that reflects the work of the people in the faith community

All five of those marks are a deliberate and ongoing part of our daily life. We are unambiguously, intentionally and unquestionably a Church!"

Notes

1. The United Church of Canada, Inter-church and Inter-faith Committee, "Prelude" from "Mending the World: An Ecumenical Vision for Healing and Reconciliation" (36th General Council, 1997), 1.

2. General Assembly Minutes, 1885, p. 390.

3. *Vancouver Herald*, April 23, 1886.

4. *Vancouver Herald*, May 21, 1886.

5. *Vancouver Historical Journal*, January 1958, vol. 1, p. 54.

6. *Vancouver Province*, June 4, 1921.

7. *Vancouver Province*, May 25, 1933.

8. Margaret A. Ecker, *National Home Monthly*, September 1937, p. 48.

9. *The World Daily*, March 29, 1922, 1.

10. Annual Report, 1924, First Presbyterian Church, BC Conference United Church Archives.

11. *National Home Monthly*, September 1937, p. 48.

12. *National Home Monthly*, September 1937, pp. 7, 46–48.

13. *Vancouver Province*, BC Magazine, December 18, 1954, p. 3.

14. Hugh Rae speech, J. Richmond Craig biography file, BC Conference United Church Archives.

15. A.B. Robertson and Mrs. Laura Miller, letters to Susan Thompson, student at Vancouver School of Theology, 1971, BC Conference United Church Archives.

16. ABC Bookworld, "Roddan, Andrew," *ABC Bookworld*, http://abcbookworld.com (accessed September 24, 2010).

17. *The New Outlook*, August 26, 1931.

18. Andrew Roddan, *God in the Jungles: The Story of a Man Without a Home* (Vancouver: First United Church, 1931).

19. Interview with Robert J. Stewart, Vancouver police chief 1980–1991, August 2010.

20. Sam Roddan, *Mind, Heart and Hand* (Vancouver: N.p.), pp. 137–8.

21. *Vancouver Sun*, July 24, 1965, p. 9.

22. The Jubilee Fund Appeal brochure, 1935.

23. Andrew Roddan, *The Church in Action: The Story of Ten Years of Active Service* (Vancouver: First United Church, n.d. [c. 1939]), p. 24.

24. *Vancouver Sun*, December 24, 1985, p. A6.

25. Sam Roddan, "Memoirs" (unpublished), BC Conference United Church Archives.

26. Eveline Freethy to Bob Stewart, 1985, BC Conference United Church Archives.

27. Interview with David Roddan, April 25, 2010.

28. Institutional Church Survey, January 1944, BC Conference United Church Archives.

29. *Vancouver Province*, April 27, 1948.

30. Individuals from this point on in are referred to by their first names because those individuals are contemporary to the author.

31. *First Things First*, vol. 4, no. 2, March 1985.

32. *First Things First*, vol. 4, no. 4, September 1985.

33. *First Things First*, vol. 4, no. 4, September 1985.

34. Glen Baker, *These Days* (Lancaster, Penn.: n.p., vol. 15, no. 3, 1985).

35. Denny Boyd, "Cool-Aid Miracle: Establishment with Longhairs," *Vancouver Sun*, November 17, 1971, p. 48.

36. *The United Church Observer*, December 1973.

37. Jack Shaver, "Inner City Vancouver," First United Church file, BC Conference United Church Archives.

38. Arthur Griffin, "The Griffins," unpublished memoirs, BC Conference United Church Archives, p. 13.

39. Marilyn Harrison, from Minutes of the Vancouver Burrard Presbytery, May 29, 2001. BC Conference United Church Archives.

40. *First Things First*, vol. 5, no. 2, April 1986.

41. "Reflections on Gandhi," *First Things First*, vol. 2, no. 1, February 1983.

42. Conversation with Henri Lock, August 2010.

43. *First Things First*, June 1989.

44. John Cashore, "My Years at First," *First Things First*, vol. 5, no. 2, April 1986.

45. *First Things First*, vol. 2, no. 1, February 1983.

46. *First Things First*, vol. 2, no. 4, October 1983.

47. *WISH Newsletter*, Spring 2010, p. 3.

48. First United Church file, BC Conference of the United Church Archives.

49. Conversation with David Hodge, May 2010.

50. *United Church Observer*, May 2003, p. 19.

51. *First Things First*, vol. 15, no. 5, November 1996.

52. *First Things First*, vol. 16, no. 2, June 1997.

53. Ruth Wright to the author, June 2010.

54. Ruth Wright to the author, June 2010.

55. *First Things First*, vol. 17, no. 4, September 1998.

56. *First Things First*, vol. 16, no. 4, September 1997.

57. *First Things First*, Extra edition, November 1999.

58. *First: A Ministry of Caring* (Vancouver: Fund-Raising Committee of First United Church, 1999).

59. *First: A Ministry of Caring* (Vancouver: Fund-Raising Committee of First United Church, 1999).

60. Conversation with Maggie Watts-Hammond, June 2010.

61. Joint Needs Assessment Report, April/May 2007.

62. Ric Matthews to the author, August 2010.

63. Ric Matthews to the author, August 2010.

64. *First Things First*, Spring edition, 2010.

Index